STANDARD LOAN

Unless recalled by another Reader
This item may be borrowed for

FOUR WEEKS

To renew, telephone:
01243 816089 (Bishop Otter)
01243 812099 (Bognor Regis)

Titles in the Special Needs in Ordinary Schools series

Meeting Special Needs in Ordinary Schools: An Overview
(2nd edition)

Assessing Special Educational Needs
Management for Special Needs
Reappraising Special Needs Education

Concerning pre- and primary schooling:

Primary Schools and Special Needs: Policy, Planning and Provision (2nd edition)

Pre-School Provision for Children with Special Needs

Encouraging Expression: The Arts in the Primary Curriculum
Improving Children's Reading in the Junior School: Challenges and Responses

Concerning secondary schooling:

Secondary Schools for All? Strategies for Special Needs
(2nd edition)

Humanities for All: Teaching Humanities in the Secondary School
Responding to Adolescent Needs: A Pastoral Care Approach
Science for All: Teaching Science in the Secondary School
Shut Up! Communication in the Secondary School

Concerning specific difficulties:

Children with Hearing Difficulties
Children with Learning Difficulties
Children with Speech and Language Difficulties
Improving Classroom Behaviour: New Directions for Teachers and Pupils

Forthcoming:

Educating the Able
Secondary Mathematics and Special Needs
Special Needs and the 1988 Act

Management for
Special Needs

Brian Walters

CASSELL

Cassell
Villiers House, 41/47 Strand,
London WC2N 5JE

387 Park Avenue South,
New York, NY 10016-8810

First published 1994

British Library Cataloguing-in-Publication Data
A catalogue record for this book is available from the British Library.

Library of Congress Cataloging-in-Publication Data
Applied for.

ISBN 0-304-32799-9

Typeset by Colset Private Limited, Singapore
Printed and bound in Great Britain by
Biddles Ltd, Guildford and King's Lynn

Contents

Acknowledgements

Acknowledgements are due to the following:

Clwyd County Council, for extensive references to *Into the Future* (County Mission Statement and Development Plan), *Handbook for Parents of Children with Special Needs*, and extracts from the Special Needs Development Plan for 1990, including Figure 7.1;

Department for Education, London, for Figures 4.2 and 7.2, from *Getting the Act Together*;

Falmer Press, for Figure 6.2, from P. Holly and G. Southworth, *Characteristics for School Development Plans: The Developing School*.

National Association for Special Needs, for Figure 4.1, from V. Gordon, *Your Primary School*;

National Union of Teachers, for Figure 5.3, from *Local Management of Schools and Special Needs*;

Parrswood High School, Manchester, for Table 7.4;

St Cloud School District, Minnesota, for Figure 7.3;

St George's School, Tunbridge Wells, for Table 7.5.

Editorial foreword

This series of books was launched in 1987 on the premise that the curriculum of all schools needed to be much more accessible to all pupils. Since then, schools have been deluged with new initiatives, Acts of Parliament, statutory orders and non-statutory guidance and constant changes of policy and practice. Are we nearer or further away from a curriculum accessible to all pupils? Will there be winners and losers? Is special needs provision in crisis?

On the positive side, a national curriculum is in place, which at least provides children with a common entitlement and teachers with a common language. Each school should now have reviewed its curriculum and its policies for pupils with special educational needs. But all this is against a background of open competition in which schools are supposed to be judged by league tables of pupil achievement, staying on and truancy rates and ability to attract additional funds. Local education authorities have been greatly weakened and no longer have the resources to co-ordinate and plan for all children in their community, though they are still responsible for children with statements of need within the framework of the Education Act 1981, which is itself being amended, and of the Children Act 1989. HMI, who have for many years provided independent national assessments of quality assurance for schools and services as a whole, are but a shadow of what they were and have lost their distinctive voice and identity within the new school inspection arrangements developed by the Office for Standards in Education. Schools largely control their own budgets and are free to set their own priorities. These may include becoming selective or specialised, excluding or including children with or without special educational needs, and finally opting for grant maintained status. In a system as diverse and divisive as this, what are the prospects for children already at the margins of society and of schools?

Where progress has been made in special needs provision, it has generally been due to well-informed and well targeted lobbying by teachers, parents and advocates who have had a clear vision of what they wanted and did not want for children. It is not enough to make a case for any group of children merely on the grounds of compassion or sympathy, or to protest when, as so often happens, they have been overlooked in the rush to reform. Official reassurances that the national curriculum is for all children, 'including those with special needs', should not be necessary. They should be included in all discussions on policy and practice, not added as an afterthought.

Against this background, Dr Walters' book could hardly be more timely, founded as it is on clear values and commitment to all pupils and building on many years of successful LEA experience. He shows that management is not a matter for heads, senior staff, governors or politicians alone but a responsibility of all members of staff, from the headteacher to the cooks and cleaners, all of whom affect and reflect the values which the school places on all its pupils. Management, in other words, is too important to be left to managers. The book provides a wealth of information on how progress can be made even within the present unfavourable climate. There are opportunities to be grasped, openings to be exploited, hearts and minds to be won, procedures to follow and committees to persuade. But success will come only if there is unity of action and purpose: above all between parents and teachers; between teachers in ordinary and special schools and those working in support services; between teachers and fellow professionals, such as educational psychologists, social workers, health professionals; and between all of these and school governors and community representatives. All of them will find Dr Walters' book a helpful guide through the maze.

Professor Peter Mittler
Manchester
June 1993

—1

Introduction to special needs management. A changing scene

A kaleidoscope dance of issues.

(with apologies to Robert Louis Stevenson)

After a decade of achievement and change in special needs education in the 1980s, the 1990s reveal that there are major reviews under way, bringing the educational spotlight clearly on to the issues surrounding special needs. These reviews, outlined in the White Paper *Choice and Diversity* (1992) and the Education Act 1993, will undoubtedly influence special needs education to the turn of the century and beyond. This book is about the management issues that need to be considered in the field of special education and it makes a timely contribution to the current debate. The author has been actively involved in various managerial capacities in special needs education for some 20 years, and in particular with implementing the changes that have taken place in the 1980s and early 1990s.

The educational changes that have taken place can vividly be seen in the range and extent of regulations and orders made in recent years. In the 43 years between 1944 and 1987, 31 statutory instruments were issued by the Department of Education and Science and the preceding Ministry of Education. Since then some 80 statutory instruments have been issued, with no sign of any abatement. In addition to this, five major Education Acts have appeared, with the latest one in 1993, containing 29 sections on special needs alone, so that one could be forgiven for being bewildered by these changes. With a further five Secretaries of State for Education since 1979 one could be excused for being 'confused'.

A CHANGE IN MANAGEMENT

During this period a new management has begun to emerge, prompted by the need for increased financial constraints, equal opportunities, calls for value for money, decentralisation, and 'getting closer to the customer'. The author was involved in the implementation of a strategic policy and programme for special needs management in the county of Clwyd over these years.

This programme identified the diverse range of knowledge, skills, experiences and personal qualities which were characteristic of effective management in special needs education at all levels. It established that individual, group and institutional needs should be identified within the context of the authority's values, and missions, setting clear aims and objectives. This called for an effective development of the county's resources and agencies to provide a variety of structured management training situations (including 'on the job', 'close to the job' and 'off the job' opportunities). One basic aim was to develop mainstream, special schools, units and support services, to work in harmony on a collective basis in order to improve their effectiveness and interrelationship so that a more efficient service was given to children with special needs, their schools and their families. It also established working partnerships between professional colleagues, governing bodies of schools, county council members, support services and the local communities.

Particular features of this collaborative approach included a shared and clear view of the county policy and strategy, the establishment of common ground and common language between the groups concerned, and the creation of an atmosphere where individual contributions were valued. Out of these management initiatives grew the concept of an integrated support service with a genuine partnership created between mainstream and special schools in developing registers of special needs. This partnership extended to the other agencies through joint care planning teams and was particularly seen in action through the All Wales strategy for mental handicap, in joint planning with other agencies including voluntary organisations, parental groups and service users. By the turn of the decade this had become well developed into an organisational value system. The managerial culture at the time regarded staff training as a major development for the future. This concentration on 'people development' enabled the educational change process of the late 1980s and early 1990s to be undertaken with some measure of success.

As a consequence of these developments, a total quality management approach was adopted in many service sectors including the schools psychological service, which was awarded a British Standard Institution BS5750 Quality Assurance Certificate. Such an approach requires a regular review of policy, a corporate attitude involving all staff, and a focus on customer needs. Overall, it emphasised the need for team work and a consistent flow of information. This was provided by weekly team meetings of central special needs management, with field meetings on a similar basis, together with an in-house magazine and a monthly newsletter on programme developments.

THE CHALLENGE OF CHANGE

Today, as the 1990s gain momentum, challenges are no less formidable, with the government claiming the White Paper 1992 'as a blueprint for the education of the future and the most significant contribution to educational progress since the 1944 Education Act'. In spite of these claims some commentators, e.g. Adamson (1992), see the new legislation as causing mayhem for special needs rather than as a blueprint for progress. In highlighting the 29 clauses of the Act concerned with special needs, he welcomes the extension of parental rights, integration and improvements in the statementing process. However, he fears that in a rapidly changing world of diminishing resources, vanishing educational bureaucracies and an increasingly competitive market-place, the negative effects will be seen in the following areas:

- a continuing increase in litigation which ultimately favours lawyers and those most used to gaining access to the legal process;
- a shift of what limited resources there are into the statementing process and away from the much larger group of children who do have special needs, but not to the extent of warranting a statement;
- preventive strategies designed to tackle special educational needs of children at an early age will be starved of cash as parents see the only way of attracting resources is the statementing process itself;
- an added incentive for schools to dump their 'problem' children into the lap of the LEA rather than devising strategies to improve behaviour within the school environment. Such children are in danger of being increasingly marginalised.

Further, as an increasing number of schools became grant-maintained, and with local management being extended to special schools by 1994, so the issues begin to accumulate. Allied to this are the plans for the redevelopment of local government in England and Wales into smaller units. With regard to special needs, a major problem is how, in a system of increasing independence of schools, can provision for the needs of small groups of special needs children be strategically managed? There is a real danger that children with special needs will be overlooked even more than they are at present and that their needs will be disregarded, or at best be given a low priority in provision. Major concerns have been expressed about the conflicting philosophies of the Education Acts 1981 and 1988 with the latter regarding the child as a unit of resource, a special needs age weighted pupil unit (SNAWPU), thereby producing a return to categorisation of pupils to fit a formula.

Thus, with the decreasing powers of LEA and the greater independence of schools, there is a need to ensure that the requirements of the Education Act 1981 for identification, assessment and provision for special needs are not disregarded. Although the White Paper 1992 recommends greater parental choice, speedier time-scales on statementing and appeals, there are no clear indications of how these factors are to be implemented and by what body. Although a Select Committee on Education is considering the difficulties of statementing at the time of writing, Baroness Warnock (1992) feels that the concept of statementing must be radically rethought.

A CHANGE IN VALUES

In the light of these issues there is a considerable need for a restatement of values and ideals in this area of education. Is integration still on the agenda as a national issue, as a legal requirement, or will it, as appears at the moment, be dependent on local or regional variations in attitudes and resources? The cry for values, such as 'equal opportunity', 'equal access' and 'each child is of equal worth', are hard to square with the increasing competition and access to schools based on key stage test results, league tables and units of resource.

The justification for the grandiose title of the Education Reform Act 1988 lies in the fact that it represents the outcomes of the reappraisal of educational values begun in the 1970s and continued with James Callaghan's Ruskin Speech of 1976, in which he shifted the educational value from educational equality to quality of educational performance and its relevance to employment. By 1986 Sir Keith Joseph's White Paper on 'Better Schools' was turning up the temperature on quality in the curriculum, so that by the time of the Education Reform Act 1988 the scene had been set and two main factors were in place to improve quality. These were namely a National Curriculum setting out what children should be taught and local management of schools, invoking Rayner/Thatcherism market forces by giving more choice for parents and more competition between schools in performance monitoring.

Values in education need to be clearly articulated, not only at the national and regional level but at the local level. What are the goals and aspirations of education for the future: are all children regarded as equal or are some more equal than others? Ball (1990, p. 14) makes the point that competition between schools is now very real, and that the ability to attract pupils will affect staff levels and the overall level of service which any school can offer. Those with decreasing numbers will lose as budgets are adjusted. In effect, the 'weak will go to the wall' and will close. Those special needs children who carry a cash incentive created by a statement may well be attractive to some schools with diminishing resources, although conversely their appearance in school performance results may lower those schools' reputation and reduce further admissions.

Tomlinson (1992) clearly shows that values drive choices, i.e. the values of the stakeholders in a school affect its policy and decisions. He feels that the value issue, if not resolved at the school, authority or national level, can become destructive. Certainly the White Paper 1992 maintains that values underline the educational system. Whatever values are left in a market economy, it is in the public service, not least the education system, where they must be realised. It is in public services where values can be added to correct the imperfections of the market. So in the field of education, equity in educational provision and services will meet those special needs that cannot be expressed in the market. As Stewart and Ranson (1988, p. 6) indicated, 'if equity is sought in the public arena then it must influence the nature of management'. A major question in this regard raised by the Select Committee on Education's review of statementing is, how can scarce resources for special needs be provided on an equitable basis and how can such distribution of resources be effectively monitored?

Stewart and Ranson raise a further value issue for education which will be considered again in Chapter 2; that is the issue of citizenship, a concept much loved by the present Prime Minister, John Major. They show that in the public domain the public are not just clients or customers of the public sector organisation, they are themselves a part of that organisation as citizens. So their citizenship can be a basic value in education, and in allowing for citizenship, educational managers have to encompass a set of relationships for which the private sector model has no place. Again, the Select Committee in addressing this issue are consulting on how parents can be included in the consultation and decision-making process on the statementing of their children. The new legislation calls for greater parental choice in the selection of special educational provision for their children. Allied to this the Children Act 1989 also gives children a greater say in decision-making about their own needs and provision.

A CHANGE TO LOCAL MANAGEMENT

Local management of schools creates a climate for greater parental choice, but this has a number of pitfalls for special needs, some of which have already been mentioned. As resources and responsibilities are delegated from the centre to the circumference, so fresh problems arise. The Audit Commission document *Losing an Empire* (1989) sees these changes as enabling LEAs to develop a new role by concentrating on leadership, mission and quality control procedures rather than handling the day-to-day affairs of schools. Clwyd in embracing this idea warmed to the new role of visionary and leader in its marketing booklet *Into the Future* (Clwyd County Council, 1989). Increased delegation took place across a number of areas as schools also warmed to their new responsibilities. The formula funding of special needs to schools was accommodated under the auspice of county special needs registers, and the budgets, as we shall see later, allocated to individual schools. Local Management of Schools for Special Schools (LMS(S)) was also trialled for implementation in 1994. However, inherent problems were detected in the LMS system as has been indicated already, and will be considered again, but sufficient to say at this stage that in spite of an encouraging culture and systematic management training there are still difficulties. These can be viewed under the following headings:

- as increasing delegation of special needs resources and manpower are made, there is less left at the centre for the LEA to use in order to monitor both the efficient and effective use of the delegated resources;
- there is no guarantee, although service contracts and agreements have been made, that schools will buy in all the available LEA provision;
- there is a danger of the dissipation of strategic well-trained skills in certain larger schools at the expense of smaller schools;
- there could be an increasing call for statements to be used as a unit of resource, with the possible transfer of children to special schools, when statements in the mainstream are too expensive to underwrite;
- under LMS(S) there might well be a restriction on integration opportunities unless special school outreach is costed as a place factor.

Housden (1992) feels that a major factor in this debate is that the national criteria for local management of schools have transferred resources away from schools serving disadvantaged areas to schools serving more advantaged communities. The requirement that 80 per cent of the total spending on schools' formula budgets should be allocated by pupil numbers has lowered the degree of positive discrimination available to LEAs. As a consequence, schools serving disadvantaged areas with a high population of vulnerable children have had a reduction in their previous special needs provision.

THE NEED FOR STRATEGIC PLANNING

In order that the competing challenges within education can be faced in this complex market environment, there is a crying need for detailed policies to be agreed at every stage in the system, but especially in strategic special needs planning and provision. Such policy documents will need wide-ranging consultation before agreement is reached by all the stakeholders involved, but they are long overdue and will require clear strategies for implementation and development, as Circular 7/91 indicates.

Such development strategies at the macro- and micro-levels are clearly on the agenda for education authorities, schools and colleges in the next few years. These development plans need to form part of a school or authority business plan and to be reflected in the annual budget, position statement and development exercise.

However, it is meaningless to create development plans that do not have clear targets and objectives which are achievable and measurable. There is now an increasing call in the 1990s for monitoring the quality in educational provision, especially with so much development now taking place at the local level, where accountability can be measured. Special needs could well benefit from the change from an authority responsibility to becoming a local school and community responsibility.

A CHANGE IN QUALITY

However, in this shift to local development there is a clear call for school performance to be measured. Parent's charters for education currently concentrate on examination results, levels of attendance, and the numbers continuing into further education, 'the out-comes' of education. But there is clearly a need to consider the effectiveness of provision for special needs children whether in the mainstream or in special schools in terms of more value added, objective, educational criteria. *Getting in on the Act* (Audit Commission, 1992a), although tested on a limited sample, felt that there was little measurable difference on their criteria of provision between special schools and mainstream schools. Clearly, value-added inputs and the processes of education also need to be considered as well as the outcomes. The report raises some key questions, particularly as to what constitutes special needs and whether the same criteria in terms of performance apply for example to schools with children with severe learning difficulties as well as schools with children with emotional and behavioural disorders. Or again, what are objective educational standards of effectiveness in these domains, when children are often said 'to be working towards Key Stage one' for most of their educational lives?

Discussion on performance by schools and of children inevitably turns its focus on teachers and questions their performance and effectiveness. Thus in the 1990s teacher appraisal is on the agenda as well as school appraisal. Can an approved system of appraisal be clearly worked out, will it be wedded to outcomes in terms of examination results, and are the input and process dimensions also worthy of consideration? Again, the differences in appraisal between a teacher of children with emotional and behavioural disorders compared with a teacher of children with severe learning difficulties could well look at different criteria. What of the appraisal process for a sixth-form teacher in a leafy suburban school, compared with a first-form teacher in an inner city school with a high proportion of special needs children? The question of who is to carry out such appraisals is still a matter for discussion and development. It is clearly not to be the new army of private inspectors under OFSTED, who will be hard pressed to report on schools every four years.

With such appraisals looming, and with the ever-increasing demands for the teacher to cope with the challenges of the curriculum, teachers could be excused if they bypass the knowledge base and take the easy way out. So to this end, with every day beginning with an act of worship, the following well-known hymn 'Jerusalem' could be sung, at least in England.

Text	*Satisfies*
And did those feet	units – maths attainment target
In ancient time	history
Walk upon England's .... mountains green?	outdoor pursuits
And was the holy Lamb of God ..	cross-curricular home economics, rural studies, RE
On England's pleasant .... pastures seen?	geography
And did the countenance .... divine	creative and expressive arts
Shine forth upon our .... clouded hills?	balanced science measurement of dew point
And was Jerusalem builded .... here	work experience
Among those dark Satanic .... mills?	moral and religious education
Bring me my bow of burning ...... gold!	balanced alchemy
Bring me my arrows of desire!	sex education
Bring me my spear! O clouds, ... unfold!	practical science – see dew point
Bring me my chariot of fire!	road safety

I will not cease from mental	personal and social
fight,	development
Nor shall my sword sleep in	active learning
my hand,	
Till we have built Jerusalem	technology
In England's green and	poetry, ecology
pleasant land.	

Please note that the above has been found wanting in sexist connotations and thus satisfies equal opportunities requirements. The process will of course satisfy the RE, English and music requirements. The teacher can then continue with the process of education, content that the National Curriculum is covered.

A book about management in education in general, or special education management in particular, must come to terms with the times and circumstances of its readers. So we need to include in our thinking all of these issues of quality management, quality assurance, performance indicators, teacher appraisal and school development. These issues need to be made clearly comprehensible in the process to the stakeholders, not least to parents, the community, and the world of business and commerce. Schools therefore need not only a development plan but also a marketing plan in which to set out their strategies and objectives in an understandable form, so that their consumers can choose the appropriate education provision and also question the goals and aspirations of the schools in their community. In a time of increasing choice in the public sector, all areas of education will need to look not only at the way they present their public image but at the way in which they present their services to a more discerning and discriminating public.

BUILDING ON GOOD PRACTICE

The Audit Commission report, *Getting the Act Together* (1992b), shows that there is clear evidence of good practice in various parts of England and Wales and some clear exemplars in other parts of the world on special education policy and practice. Many LEAs and special schools have developed some excellent provisions, which must be seen beside some rather negative responses given by the survey. Indeed in recent years HMI have identified many areas of good practice over a range of special needs issues, such as curriculum differentiation and development, support service provision, levels of integration and opportunities for continuing education in special needs, to name a few. There has been a plethora of reporting of good practice of mainstream schools in integrating a range of special needs children from the blind to the dyslexic, with a wealth of information available on early intervention programmes and inter-agency co-operation in networking for special needs support.

In the course of this book, the intention is to draw upon this good practice with examples of the provision that is taking place in local authorities, schools or services and to illustrate the management practices which are found therein. If a whole school approach to integration or differentiation of the curriculum is considered, then practical demonstrations will be given of its outworking in a particular school. Similarly, if outreach from a special school is seen to be good practice and part of a marketing scheme in offering a special school's expertise to the mainstream, then this will be used as an illustration of useful practice. Wherever possible, therefore, not only relevant theory but relevant practice will be considered.

The book follows a developmental pattern of management in special needs by looking first at the core philosophy and values in the system, whether derived from legislation or accepted principles; and second, at how such values and beliefs are translated into concepts and statements of mission for a school, service and authority. How such mission statements in special needs education are then translated into policy documents, and how such policy documents are delivered and communicated, is the next area for investigation. Consideration of how such policy is put into practice is made through development plans, containing aims, objectives and clear criteria for performance monitoring and quality control. Finally, how will these plans result in schools and services marketing their programmes to their 'customers'?

In conclusion, the Audit Commission document *Getting the Act Together* (1992b) devoted some considerable prominence to the special needs management developments in the Clwyd Authority, also highlighted by the *Times Educational Supplement* (13 November 1992), as examples of good practice. If I refer to these developments from time to time in this book, I hope the reader will forgive my indulgence.

Educational values and special needs

A system at ease with itself?

(with apologies to John Major)

THE CALL FOR EQUAL RIGHTS

Special needs value statements have been much in evidence in the last 20 years. The United Nations (1975), in its *Declaration of the Rights of the Disabled*, made the following statement:

> Whatever the origin, nature or seriousness of their handicaps and disabilities, disabled people have the same fundamental rights as their fellow citizens of the same age which implies first and foremost the right to a decent life as normal and as full as possible.

In the United States in the 1980s the Public Law PL94142 legislated on educational access, individualised educational programmes and integration at the state and local school district levels for students with special needs. Similarly, other countries such as Denmark and Sweden have approached the comprehensive school model of equal access and integration for special needs children.

In the United Kingdom, the Warnock Report (DES, 1978, 1.4) maintained that 'the purpose of education for all children is the same, the goals are the same, but the help that individual children need in progressing towards them will be different'.

VALUES IN THE PUBLIC SECTOR

Decisions made in the public sector are value laden; the achievement of collective values is the purpose of the public domain, so that management in that domain has to be sensitive to the values inherent in its actions, for if it is not, it denies the purpose of the public sector.

As these values are patterned by social, economic and political relationships, such values as economy and efficiency became prominent in the 1980s because the public sector was seen to be a burden on the economy. As a consequence, public expenditure needed to be held back so that the private sector could have room to expand. There was the growing political force of neo-liberalism which was an important strand in the success of Rayner–Thatcherism in the United Kingdom and Reaganism in the United States. This neo-liberalism, which generally belonged to the Conservative party, emphasised individual freedom and decentralisation and sought to limit the scope and power of the state. However, this was not the only ideology present in central or local government, particularly in the larger metropolitan authorities of local government. The varying ideologies and value systems of the 1980s and early 1990s can be seen in Table 2.1.

Value systems are at the heart of management in both the public and private sectors. Amongst the key criteria for successful companies enunciated by Peters and Waterman (1982) are attention to the organisations' values system and centralisation through a system of shared values. The idea of shared values is at the core of any successful management (see Figure 2.1).

EDUCATION AND VALUES

The 1992 White Paper states clearly that education cannot and must not be value-free, and that a set of shared values should be at the heart of every school's educational and pastoral policy and practice. Furthermore, every attempt should be made to ensure that these values are endorsed by parents and the local community.

The problem of course is who will articulate these values, and are the same spiritual, moral and cultural beliefs shared by all in a pluralistic society? To some extent the White Paper considers that values are to be found by having a proper regard to the nation's Christian heritage and traditions. It is apposite to consider that there is a call to religious values, as found in the Victorian value system, by the current Secretary of State for Education, John Patten. Indeed, there has been a regular call from the political right in recent years for a return to Victorian values. The opening quotation in the White Paper is from John Ruskin (1862), with a call for equal opportunities for all children so that they might be educated on equal terms.

A RETURN TO VICTORIAN VALUES

What are these values, and do we still hold them dear today? The message of Ruskin's time was that human failure was often rooted in personal moral weakness and it called upon people to practise hard

Table 2.1 *Five ideologies of local government*

Ideology	Neo-liberal new right	Conservative new right	Left statist	New urban left	Communitarian
Sees principal role of local government as:	To serve the local community	As an agent of parliament and central government welfare state services	Social citizenship: to deliver high-quality uniform service	To serve the community	To serve the local community
Illustrative policy	Community charge	Urban corporations	Comprehensive education	Enterprise boards	Local income tax
Dominant values	Liberty, choice, efficiency economy	Public order, discipline, efficiency, reduced public expenditure	Social citizenship, equality of service provision	Citizen participation in a widened political process. Redistribution of opportunities/life changes	Participation, localism

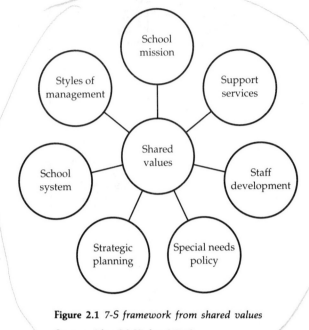

Figure 2.1 *7-S framework from shared values*

Source: After McKinley (1977)

work, persistence, will-power and individual effort. These criteria could be based on purely secular foundations such as the Samuel Smiles 'self-help' philosophy, but they also coincided with the beliefs and attitudes of Christian evangelicalism. Thus individualism and self-interest were firmly on the Victorian agenda. Yet at the same time, at least for the middle classes, there was a call to duty, caring for the poor, the provision of charity, and the growth of voluntary societies. In fact, in 1872, at the funeral of Lord Shaftesbury, a principal leader of the evangelicals in public life, there were representatives of nearly 500 such voluntary societies. However, Victorian evangelicalism did not seek changes in the social structure; in fact it not only stressed individual responsibility for poverty but it also encouraged a humble acceptance of a social order where a hierarchy of rich and poor was divinely ordained. This was given classic expression in a verse of the popular hymn 'All Things Bright and Beautiful', written in 1849 by Mrs C.F. Alexander, the wife of the Archbishop of Dublin:

> The rich man in his castle,
> The poor man at his gate,
> God made them high and lowly,
> And ordered their estate.

In this environment, education, which had its roots in the provision for an élite, although becoming increasingly available to all, preserved the opportunities for such an élite in separate institutions. As Housden (1992, p. 8) suggests, right up to the present day there is a tendency in certain parts of society to view education as something that really matters in its highest embodiment to only a very few. It then becomes somehow excusable to 'short-change' some children.

However, there were other voices and important strands to Victorian social thought. There was a call for the development of equal rights and equal opportunity with Christian socialism by Anglicans such as F. D. Maurice in the late 1850s, and this movement made significant contributions to Victorian working-class life and organisation through the co-operative movement and the founding of working men's colleges such as Ruskin College. Later in the period, groups such as the Christian Social Union and the Guild of St Matthew advocated much greater state intervention and legislation to overcome poverty, and these groups saw the problem of the working class more in terms of social conditions and less in terms of personal responsibility or moral failure. These ideas are echoed in our time in the Anglican tradition by David Sheppard in his book *Bias to the Poor* (1983).

CURRENT ISSUES IN PUBLIC VALUES FOR SPECIAL NEEDS

In the twentieth century, there has been a steady growth of equal rights and equal opportunities across race, religion, gender and, more recently, handicap. Today, most employers regard themselves as equal opportunity employers, certainly in the public sector. Throughout the industrialised nations there has been a development of the equal opportunities issue in terms of wages, opportunities and access. Public laws now make it illegal in many countries to discriminate on the basis of race or gender, so enabling the establishment public watchdog committees and commissions for equal opportunities and race relations. In this environment, the Warnock Committee deliberated on the concept of special needs education in the United Kingdom in the late 1970s. The concept of normalisation, equal opportunity, integration and equal access was given expression in the Warnock Report on special needs and was paralleled in most of Western Europe and the United States in a period stretching from the mid-1960s to the mid-1980s. During the 1980s the values of equal opportunity for all and equal access were given fuller expression with the Education Reform Act 1988 in advocating equal access to a common curriculum for all.

VALUES FOR A POST-INDUSTRIAL SOCIETY

Greater acceptance of the handicapped has been facilitated by economic growth which has allowed more funding to be reserved for such needs without taking funds from already established services. This is clearly apparent in a country like Norway, with the boom created by North Sea oil and a consequent large-scale funding in support for the handicapped special needs population. However, it is fair to say that in many ways our society still reflects the values of the industrial revolution. Economic productivity is the primary basis for employment and as such is a focal point in the individual's relationship with society and a major source of self-esteem. On this analysis, the criteria for judging the quality of education is its effectiveness in preparing the child for employment. Ever since the industrial revolution our basic targets have centred on material growth, and our value system to a large extent has reflected these goals. As we enter a post-industrial society there is still a hyper-expansionist vision: the 'HE society' as it is sometimes called, a society whose values are geared to quantitative goals, money values and centralising strategies, both intellectual and rational. This has largely been the spirit of the Thatcher 'yuppie' years, with an abundance of goods and services that have undoubtedly improved the quality of life. In such a society with such values, education will continually be to prepare young people for a full-time job. Its main aims will be to provide them with the credentials to obtain and hold down a job and to socialise them into what will remain a full employment, mass consumption society. The main criteria of a good education will be the certificates, diplomas and attainment targets that one can show for it and the jobs which these qualifications open up. The current climate in the early 1990s, even with high unemployment amongst young school leavers, cultivates this ideal and these values. However, education could be said to be dividing into two branches: the first qualifies people for high-status jobs as members of a professional technocratic elite; the second is increasingly teaching people how to use their leisure, with a lower status outcome from their education.

However, the negative side-effects of economic growth have resulted in environmental damage which has affected the quality of air and water, with natural resources being depleted. Thus concentration on such issues as the ozone layer, global warming and the rain forests has been to the fore in the public arena, with the first world conference on ecological conservation in 1992 in Brazil. So reactions against such negative effects may indicate in future years that our value system is changing. Although President Bush was seen in the 1992 election year as more concerned with unemployment in Detroit than rain forests in Brazil, his successor President Clinton's mission has the watchword 'everybody counts', although it is not clear whether this applies to Detroit or to Brazil.

We are perhaps on the verge of a more radical look at our post-industrial society, working towards a more sane, humane and ecological (SHE)-based set of values, where qualitative goals are on the agenda. Such qualities as personal growth and interpersonal values may well be given greater emphasis in education towards all-round competence and self-reliance, with an emphasis on 'feminine' priorities of intuition and empathy and on localisation rather than centralisation. In educational terms this could be education for capability, with an emphasis on learning life skills and geared to a life-style in which people expect to have part-time employment and at the same time undertake a good deal of useful rewarding activity for themselves and their neighbours. Such a value system may recognise that people often learn better from doing things with experienced people, so that trainee teachers are in the classroom rather than receiving classroom instruction from professional educators in a university or college.

Clearly, as we progress through the 1990s, many of these values become mixed and cross-fertilised. Certainly in many ways the National Curriculum is geared to academic and technical attainment, preparing people for the world of full-time work, with a strong competitive edge in pursuing certificates and diplomas. However, learning for living and educating for life is also on the educational agenda, particularly in the area of special needs. The problem at the moment is that everyone wants to qualify for high-status jobs, and in a climate of equal opportunity and still equal worth, those with special needs want to be included in the race. The trouble with racing is that there are winners and losers.

Changes in values away from economic factors could have a number of implications for handicapped individuals. An emphasis on self-actualisation of individuals and concentration on normalisation, as outlined by Wolfsenberger (1972), could reinforce the idea of educating every handicapped person to their maximum potential. In a devolved educational system, such concentration on self-actualisation could bring about less emphasis on vocational economically productive training and more emphasis on those areas of learning aimed at life skills and enriching the life of the individual through art and music for a fuller participation in society and culture. The normalisation movement and care-in-the-community programmes have seen the transfer of handicapped persons from long-stay institutions to community-based facilities, with the forming of stronger community ties and with less alienation and more normal social relationships developing.

A CLASH OF VALUES

However, the current economic value system has collided with an economic slow-down in progress and productivity at the beginning of the 1990s. At both international and national levels, this has led to an increase in conflict and competitiveness, with individuals being increasingly concerned with their own interests. This is certainly having a negative impact on the special needs population. Such a competitive society most often advocates the survival of the fittest with the weak going to the wall, and there is little sympathy currently for steps that might increase the economic competitive advantage of the special needs population through positive discrimination.

Yet in spite of this competitive market approach there has been talk in the early 1990s of the values enshrined in the idea of citizenship and of active and responsible citizenship. Citizen's charters abound, and are found in education for special needs. However, as education is becoming subordinated in many aspects to a competitive market, so also the citizen's powers are being undermined. We see already that parental choice in schooling in many parts of the country is being eroded by over-competitive schools and schools becoming selective. Yet there is an attempt in the White Paper 1992 to give increased rights to parents on the choice of schools for their children with special needs in the statementing process. Nevertheless, this is already causing problems for those parents seeking places in over-subscribed schools, which are 'drowning in the sea of their own popularity'.

CITIZENSHIP AND VALUES

'Ideas of civic activity, public spiritedness and participation in a community of equals', says Chantal Mouffe, 'are alien to most neo liberal thinkers. They consider them as pre-modern and that such ideas as the common good and civic duty should be rejected' (1988, p. 28). Thus liberal individualism, which is the cause of the increasing lack of social cohesion in democratic societies, has undermined feelings of common purpose, obligation and community values. Such liberals argue that these ideas are incompatible with the pluralisms of modern democracies. According to them, ideas of the common good today can only have totalitarian consequences. Mouffe (1988) makes the point 'that democratic citizenship however is an alternative strategy for modern society'. It is inspired by a view of politics and citizenship, which assumes a community of equals who share rights and social responsibility with the common ends of freedom and equality for all. This is a far cry from the Victorian and Thatcherite view of citizenship, which is a privatised conception that whisks away the notion of political community.

The current neo-liberal reduction of the common good to a question of wealth creation, taxpayers' freedom and efficiency, has been made possible by the liberals' exclusive concern with individuals and their rights at the expense of the community. Halsey (1993) considers that this liberal emphasis on individualism is a root cause of family break-down and a major factor in the decline of moral values. He describes Margaret Thatcher as a 'major architect of the demolition of the tradi-tional family' by failing to understand that such economic liberalism favouring the individual would move marriage towards a commercial contract to be ended at the convenience of either party.

Mouffe (1988, p. 31) feels that the Thatcherite and post-Thatcherite crusade for social responsibility and its privatised nature of individual citizenship should be opposed. The solution to citizenship is not to revive the Victorian feeling of *noblesse oblige* and moral duty among the rich, but to attend to our obligations as fellow members of a political community, to the rights of citizenship, thus establishing that, as citizens, we do not only have political rights but also economic and social rights. It is the ethics of the political that are at stake. The implications for special needs education in these ideas are consider-able. Maclure (1990) feels that, although the past 15 years have seen a shift away from concerns about equity and fairness and a concentra-tion on efficiency, it is difficult to believe that hopes of 'one nation' have been permanently shelved. Indeed, the present Prime Minister, John Major, has gone on record as saying that 'he is seeking to create a classless society'.

A CALL FOR A RESTATEMENT OF EDUCATIONAL VALUES

Equity, fairness, equal opportunity and equal access still remain in the educational thinking of most educationalists as necessary values and ideals. Certainly, whilst they remain, in whatever form, there is a role for local authorities to act as leaders and missionaries for promoting such ideals and values in their educational constituencies, as the Audit Commission (1989) clearly stated.

For too long the educational profession has been reluctant to state its value system, perhaps stemming from the belief that we all shared the same values and that therefore they could safely remain tacit. It is clear that the process of education is a value-laden activity, and can only be meaningful if it is based upon shared values.

The values in an educational system are very often found within the hidden curriculum. Such values enshrine the ideas that the educa-tion of every child is of equal value or of equal worth, and that all children are entitled to equality of treatment. This treatment is concerned with educating the whole person, the emotional as well as the intellectual, the spiritual as well as the academic; ideas that are enshrined in the Education Acts 1944 and 1988.

Most educators would also be committed to high expectation for pupils, teachers and schools, and for education and performance to be of a high quality; further, that schools become guidance communities committed to care and guidance and that all staff concerned should be extended professionals, dedicated to the pursuit of improvement to the highest level of their own capabilities.

Such values may be seen to be of general acceptance and to cover all children and schools. However, the concept of equal value and equal worth could well be developed into the idea that all children should be educated with their peers in their local school; that is the idea of integration at the heart of the Warnock report. One could extend this to the idea of inclusion, as articulated by Flynn (1990), that only one quality system of education should exist, rather than a mainstream system and a special system. His argument is that in a modern society which demands qualifications and credentials acquired through the education system, to be excluded from the ordinary system is the ultimate in non-achievement. One could make the point that with a National Curriculum in England and Wales common to all sectors of the educational system, this makes the special school into an ordinary school. However, occupational success, social mobility, privilege and advancement are legitimised by the education system, and for those who receive their education in a special school it could be argued that there is the possibility they may be, by and large, excluded from these things.

A PLEA FOR SPECIAL NEEDS TO BE VALUED

Flynn (1990) makes the point that special education as it has developed over the past hundred years has acted as a safety valve for ordinary education, in that certain children could be legally excluded and placed in a different system and legitimised by categorisation. So the special education system became legitimised as a permanent sub-system of the ordinary education system. It could be suggested that what is required is a system that does not deny differences between children, but one that recognises and accommodates such differences.

The Labour Party policy document for special needs (Labour Party, 1992) clearly shows that, rather than integration being part of the central policies of British education in recent years, it is separateness that characterises much of the provision for those with special educational needs. It suggests that the Education Reform Act 1988 addressed special needs only as an afterthought and that some of its central provisions may well inhibit the important good practice developed since the 1981 Act in England and Wales.

One of the major issues raised by the Audit Commission document *Getting in on the Act* (1992a) has been the lack of resources for children with special needs and that statements have very often been related to resources. At this time of special education development, there is concern that an objective view needs to be made on what constitutes 'needs'. As Stewart and Ranson have said, 'The budget in public services is an act of political choice' (1988, p. 14).

VALUES AND NEEDS

Scarce resources 'have to be fitted to meet un-met need'. That involves collective choice both in the definition of need and in the allocation of resources to need, the point being that 'need' is the most appropriate criterion for public services. But some clearer definition of the term 'need' is required. The 1981 Act states that 'a child has special educational needs if he or she has a significantly greater learning difficulty than children of his or her own age'. But this is a very vague definition and can be seen to vary according to different settings or circumstances. The diverse rates of statementing in the school population of between 0.8 per cent and 3.8 per cent between authorities clearly shows that either scarce resources are being fitted to needs or there are differing thresholds of needs.

The concept of need can be constructed in a variety of ways: one can distinguish between expressed need, felt need and normative need. Expressed need is indistinguishable from demand, although in terms of the individual this is clearly felt and communicated. There are many cases of parental requests for services/provision for their children which have been overturned by appeal, and which can be considered in this category.

Felt need exists prior to communication or action. I may feel my child has special needs but I may be frightened or unable to express that need out of respect for those in authority. English may not be my first language, or I may not know how to express my need.

Normative need is more akin to our debate as it involves an output, something measurable, observable. Most often a professional, teacher or educational psychologist, is defining need and what is needed. Teachers often label children as 'disruptive or maladjusted', when the parents may argue that the child is bored at school and what he needs is a more stimulating education. It is fair to say that the same end to meet needs is often in education achievable by a variety of means. Needs are about ends and there is room for debate about the best way of meeting them. As a consequence, if a need is an end then to say a need must be met is ultimately a value judgement and therefore special educational need is inherently value-laden.

Most of the value judgements in special needs are shared, but not always so; some may say 'that special needs are not found in the child, but in the school', as Rutter *et al.* (1979) clearly showed. The child who is bored does not need to see an educational psychologist; he needs more challenging teaching. From this perspective, needs become a feature of our social norms and culture.

Flynn's (1990) inclusion philosophy, where all children have needs, regards needs merely as a matter of degree, but considers that all such needs should be provided for in the mainstream. Using the curriculum criteria, what children need is a curriculum so differentiated that it meets their needs, so the problem from this perspective lies not in the child but with the curriculum.

It is clear, as Housden points out, that 'value questions are at the heart of any debate about needs in public education' (1992, p. 21). In a democracy, the providers and consumers of education require a social forum to argue out collectively these value questions and to monitor their articulation in policy terms. Most Western societies are committed to positive discrimination towards children with special needs, whatever the definition of need. This discrimination is seen in terms of equal access, equal opportunity and in the concept of integration. Such ideas are translated into value statements and incorporated into mission policies. However, these values may appear to be mere rhetoric to some and to be unattainable in the current climate of competition in the public sector.

VALUES AND THE PUBLIC INTEREST

To summarise: there is a major problem facing public services in the 1990s and education and special education in particular. A key issue is whether there remains a public interest over and above that of the market: that is the issue of citizenship. The struggle between the ethic of the market-place and the ethic of citizenship will continue, and how it is resolved, whether in special needs education or elsewhere, will determine the kind of society in which we live as we approach the end of this century, and whether such a society will be 'at ease with itself'.

—3—
Mission statements

Every child a special child.

(Labour Party, 1991)

MISSION AND VALUES

Values need to be expressed not so much as beliefs and ideals but as a basis for action. For ideals to be realised, a sense of purpose and activity needs to be formalised in the concept of mission. Most businesses are now developing statements of mission in which the company's ideals and beliefs are put into place as a statement of intent of action. Mission statements need not be long; they may only encompass a phrase or series of phrases and may well only cover one side of an A4 page. Whatever their expression, they should enshrine the beliefs and values of the organisation. Local education authorities, schools and services can develop statements of mission to which the varying stakeholders in the organisation can give adherence and acceptance. Without such a sense of mission, members of an organisation have no feeling of belonging, no purpose, identity or goals. With such a mission where there is common acceptance, managers and employees alike share a common purpose.

So mission statements have become a priority in the 1990s. My local gas company has issued a customer mission statement on its *raison d'être* for being in business, with the customer being at the forefront of the mission statement. Almost every large company has issued its manifesto or mission statement in recent years. Local government departments, education departments, schools colleges and universities are also being alerted to the concept of mission.

There is a move by IBM, the world's largest computer company, to offer even the smallest primary school in the United Kingdom US-style management techniques. According to Dore (1993), the American company has already piloted its work in United Kingdom schools. IBM consultant Roger Thomas considers the first step to a successful school is the mission statement, which to some may sound more like the Salvation Army than IBM, but is really what the school is about and where it needs to go. First, Thomas feels the school management needs to identify what makes the school tick, the critical success factors (CSFs) and the key operating processes (KOPs). Finally these are combined to produce the most critical processes (MCPs) and agreed quality improvement projects (AQIPs). This may all seem rather jargonistic. However, the final stage of the process is the whole team approach, where every member of staff is encouraged to have a common goal, with everyone pulling towards the same objective.

So what is a mission statement? Do we need them in the field of special needs and do they arise naturally out of our stated values?

THE NATURE OF MISSION STATEMENTS

A mission statement reveals the long-term mission of an organisation, what it wants to be and who it wants to serve. This is a declaration of an organisation's 'reason for being'. Such a statement is widely regarded by managers as the first step in strategic management. Organisations need a mission statement to ensure unanimity of purpose, to provide a basis or standard for allocating organisational resources, and to establish an organisational culture and climate.

Such a statement gives an organisation the opportunity to specify its goals and objectives and to translate these into targets so that cost, time and performance parameters can be monitored, assessed and controlled. It also enables individuals to identify with the organisation's purpose and direction and to some extent deter those who cannot so identify from participating in the organisation's activities. It usually becomes quite clear, when one is interviewed for a post in any organisation, as to what are the organisation's purpose and goals. So the *Guardian* (27 May 1990), in drawing attention to the Church of England adopting business methods, asked the question, 'will the clergy whose vision does not fit in with the diocesan mission statement, have their contracts renewed or want to stay?'.

Mission statements further facilitate the translation of objectives into a work structure, involving the assignment of tasks to responsible elements within the organisation. They also serve the purpose of specifying an organisation's purposes and provide a basis for the translation of these purposes into objectives in such a way that costs, time and performance parameters can be assessed and controlled. Figure 3.1 demonstrates the flow from mission to performance.

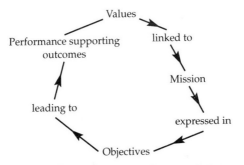

Figure 3.1 *From mission to performance indicators*

DEVELOPING MISSION STATEMENTS

In developing a mission statement, representative members of an authority, school or service will need to engage in debate in considering the key elements in formulating such a mission statement. As a consequence of the changes brought about by the Education Reform Act 1988 and the Audit Commission document 1989, *Losing an Empire, Finding a Role*, such a debate was undertaken in Clwyd by the education management team, headteachers and County Council members, facilitated by representative from Coopers & Lybrand management consultants.

The Audit Commission paper (1989) saw the LEA of the future amongst other things as being a visionary leader, articulating the mission of what the education service is trying to achieve. Within this visionary role there is a need to set clear policy statements for the future for those services for which it has responsibility. Amongst the elements of such a future mission there needs to be consideration of the context in which schools and services operate and a setting of guidelines on co-operation and continuity between schools. Other issues for focus would be the efficient use of resources, the setting up and monitoring of standards and developing criteria for the effectiveness of schools and services. Further, it suggested that the authority can, through its mission strategy, take the lead by promoting links between the community, schools, business and the other services available for children and families.

The analysis in Clwyd took place over a period of several weeks, using concentrated activities to consider the authority's basic responsibilities and the climate or culture in which these responsibilities should be carried out. The sessions took the form of 'brainstorms' where various groups considered the main issues which concerned the workings of the education service. Statements of intent were generated from these groups, which were ranked in orders of priority by all the groups concerned. This resulted, in time, with a refinement of the key factors, which were recorded on large sheets of paper. The groups were as mixed as possible, in that they did not reflect one particular constituency opinion. As a result of this period of debate and consideration, a statement of intent was developed which attempted to cover all aspects of the service that schools and the community would expect in terms of quality, commitment and excellence. This became the mission statement which was made available to all sectors of the education service including school governors and parents. This statement was incorporated in the county booklet *Into the Future* (Clwyd County Council, 1989), which included sections on shared values and the county business development plan across all sectors for the following four years, and the lifetime of the ruling administration.

The key elements highlighted in this mission statement of particular concern for special needs were that 'within schools and colleges teachers will resolve':

- to value all young people equally;
- to be concerned for the education of the whole person;
- to foster positive attitudes to the needs and wishes of the service's clients, encouraging the widest access possible to learning and removing barriers for those with special needs;
- the provision of equitable resources staffing and premises to achieve maximum benefit for all children;
- to prepare young people for citizenship in a democracy through working interactively with the local neighbourhood and the wider community.

Of course, underlying the mission statement are those values which the authority, school or service have agreed to uphold. These might include values concerned with respect and care for others, social responsibility, a sense of community, self-respect and a commitment to learning.

MISSION STATEMENTS FOR SPECIAL NEEDS

Since the publication of the Warnock Report in 1978, there have been a series of visionary statements which contain key mission criteria published at the national and local level in the United Kingdom. The report of the Fish Committee of the Inner London Education Authority, *Educational Opportunities for All* (Fish, 1986), set out some basic mission criteria for special needs education. Its major principles enshrined the idea that the aims of education for children with disabilities and significant difficulties would be the same as those for all children. To reach these aims, children and young people should be afforded equal access to all aspects of education with the recognition that integration in society is a process, not a state. This process, the report considered, should be actively encouraged wherever the individual lives and should form an essential element in all education where it takes place. The implications for these values in developing a mission statement for special needs became clear, so that the report highlighted a number of important consequences which could be summarised as a mission in the following way:

- attitudes, arrangements and approaches in schools should be changed to reduce those barriers which may have handicapping effects;
- the early involvement of the family and the individual with supporting agencies for advice and provision should be made so that they can make informed choices on the best ways to minimise handicapping effects;
- the development of service provision to support the individual in the full range of educational and social facilities;
- the long-term planning of provision for such services over all phases of life and education.

All of these mission items were articulated in a policy strategy for development for the future. This was not fulfilled however, because ILEA met its demise with the onset of the 1988 Education Reform Act.

EXAMPLES OF MISSION STATEMENTS IN SPECIAL NEEDS

Some of the basic principles and procedures from the Fish Report (1986) have clearly found their way into many other local authority mission statements. Among the principles articulated by Northamptonshire County Council (1992b), for example, which are incorporated in their mission, was an emphasis on the aims of education being the same for all pupils with a concentration on provision in the mainstream school. The segregation of an individual from the local community setting, it was emphasised, may diminish the quality of experience for the whole community. Integration would be based on shared experiences and this would apply to all pupils, whatever their educational needs, as it would to all teachers. Entitlement to the consortium of provision should not be dependent on where a pupil lived. Finally every school and teacher must play their part in identifying, assessing and monitoring individual pupils' needs.

These principles and values would need to be reflected in school and service policy statements, and the local authority would need to ensure through its monitorial and quality control procedures that this mission is effectively implemented.

Before the 1992 election, the Labour Party, in its document *Every Child a Special Child* (1991), outlined its mission with the words:

> equality requires that every child and adult be treated as having equal worth. We do not expect or want everyone to be the same, but we do want every child to have similar opportunities in life so that each can lead its life to the full.

It goes on to talk at length about access, entitlement, integration, and quality education for all, with special needs being considered at every level of policy development rather than as an afterthought, as has so often been the experience in recent years.

The idea of mission may appear pretentious to some people's ears, but it is now seen as a fundamental precursor to quality improvement in most organisations. It simply sets out in a clear, concise way what the school, service or organisation is there to do and what it is trying to achieve. It establishes a standard so that quality of provision and service can be measured.

A further example can be seen in the Saint Paul Education District, Minnesota, USA, where the public schools mission set out the following factors.

- Education mirrors the nature of society even as educational institutions and educators help shape the nature of society;
- the quality of education is the mutual responsibility of professional educators, community members, parents, learners and elected officials, each of whom have obligations which they must meet for the educational system to work effectively as a whole system for the benefit of learners and society;
- the quality of life in our community and the larger society are ultimately linked to what learners bring to, experience, and take away from the public schools.

Therefore, the mission of the Saint Paul public schools is that education shall be lifelong learning for a just, democratic and productive society. Fulfilment of the mission demands that learners, the community and the Saint Paul public schools work together. (See Table 3.1 for a development of this mission.)

MAJOR PRACTICAL CONSIDERATIONS FOR MISSION STATEMENTS

In conclusion, some practical steps in writing a mission statement are suggested which could be applied to a school or special needs support service. The statement should reflect those key factors which can be

Table 3.1 *Saint Paul public schools' mission statement*

The Saint Paul public schools

MUST BE
- Excellent
- Achievement oriented
- Equitable
- Responsive
- Appreciative of diversity
- Resourceful and cost efficient
- Supportive of community and parental goals and values
- Partners with parents and guardians in all that we do
- In compliance with applicable laws and standards

MUST PROVIDE
- A safe and nurturing environment
- Excellent academic programs in all schools
- Program choice
- Integrated learning experience
- Appropriate, individual learning programs
- Openness and responsiveness to the community
- Competent, conscientious, creative, diverse staff
- Educational leadership and accountability
- Responsible fiscal management
- Ways for schools, families, the community, business and labor, and elected officials to work together

Learners in the Saint Paul public schools

WILL EXPERIENCE
- Joy of learning
- Appropriate relevant academic challenges and successes
- Competence
- Sense of personal worth
- Know how to learn
- Confidence in applying their knowledge and skills
- Ability to work with others
- Appreciation of diversity

MUST
- Be present
- Be responsible
- Be willing to ask for and to give help
- Be prepared to learn
- Do their best
- Be respectful and honest
- Be prepared for further education and the world of work

The community, all of us together,

MUST BE COMMITTED TO
- Equality of opportunity
- Democratic values and processes
- Opportunities for all to reach their own individual potential
- Teaching good citizenship
- Respect for diversity in an integrated setting

MUST PROVIDE
- Funding for staff and resources to support lifelong learning
- Support for learners
- Respect for school staff and parents
- A political climate supporting public education
- Guidance on educational priorities
- Opportunities for gainful employment

seen as characterising the service or school to its community and constituency, specifying the provision made or service provided. A statement of the commitment to a quality service and identification of its client group within special needs should also be made. Such a statement will also serve as a criteria for policy-making for special needs provision. Wherever practicable the mission statement should reflect the rights and requirements of all the stakeholders in the educational process and motivate and challenge all those involved, giving a sense of vision for the future. If such a statement is to be practical, then all of those who are to implement it should be involved in its development, so that it can be more easily transmitted into a policy for action.

The mission statement of the learning support service (LSS) developed by the Cheshire authority (1992) embraces most of these criteria as outlined below.

- the LSS exists to provide a coherent but flexible response to the needs of children, families and professionals, so that children with special educational needs are integrated with their peers and have access to the whole curriculum;
- the service will be delivered through the following effective teams:
-   i) district learning support teams – supporting mainstream schools and individual pupils with learning difficulties through clearly defined procedures in line with the Warnock assessment stages;
- ii) the services of hearing impairment and visual impairment – working across all sectors – in the assessment and support for individual children from birth to age 19 with sensory impairments;
- iii) the service for micro-technology and SEN – working across all sectors in the assessment and provision of micro-technological equipment for pupils with SEN;
- iv) the service for traveller education – providing support to schools' traveller children and their families.
- we are committed to honesty and responsibility in all our work and respect the right of individuals to make their own informed choices. We will positively promote the practice of working as partners with families and other carers;
- we will offer families and schools professional advice and support including comprehensive assessment procedures, individual educational programmes, direct teaching, curriculum modification and differentiation and learning materials;
- we will provide a team of professional staff who are committed to continual appraisal, who are supported to further their own professional development;
- we will provide quality training opportunities for all our clients so as to enhance their skills in meeting the individual needs of children;
- we will facilitate collaboration with other supporting agencies, to ensure a consistent service to all our clients;
- we will provide the LEA with advice and information regarding the nature and levels of special needs across the authority to assist them in their forward planning, policy-making and in meeting their statutory duties;

- we will manage resources to ensure a fair and consistent distribution and maximum educational benefit for individual pupils;
- we will adopt a philosophy of continuous improvement and evaluation of every aspect of our work.

Ultimately, the values and aims of a mission statement for special needs will be expanded in a policy strategy. The means by which this policy should be implemented will need to be clearly stated to all those concerned with education and its related services and all those responsible for any form of special provision in a local authority, school or service setting.

—4—

Policy development

Without a policy the people perish.

INTRODUCTION: THE NEED FOR POLICY

The need for strategic management in the formulation of policy is an overwhelming task facing special education in the next five years.

Over recent years, since the introduction of the Education Act 1981, there has been some progress made in the developing of local education policies of special needs, with integration firmly at the centre. The Centre for Studies on Integration (1991), for example, has reviewed the progress made in this area. However, responses have been patchy and uncoordinated so that the extent of integration has varied from a significant increase in some areas to greatly increased segregation in other areas. Statementing 'time lags' also vary from six months to two years to 'no students' at all, depending on the LEA studied. As a consequence, Circular 7/91 from the DES on *Local Management of Schools* (DES, 1991a) stresses the need for revised policy documents on special needs for all LEAs, insisting that they reflect the positive changes that have taken place since the implementation of the 1981 Act and the changes demanded by the 1988 Act. Any agreed programmes for local management of special schools or services by the DES will be contingent on 'acceptable' policy documents being submitted by LEAs on their special needs strategy. There are clear guidelines in this circular for the drawing up of policy statements by local authorities. Nonetheless, Section 2(4) of the Education Act 1981 already required LEAs to keep under review the arrangements made by them for special education. Circular 7/91 makes it clear that such arrangements can only be delivered effectively if there is a clear policy made available to all the involved parties.

ISSUES IN POLICY FORMULATION

The major factors that Circular 7/91 suggests and that need to be included in such a policy document include identification of special needs and the roles of the different type of schools, including placements in independent and non-maintained and hospital settings. Further factors needing policy decisions are coordination between agencies, availability of support services, the arrangements for monitoring schools and service performance, and an overview of the provision specified in statements, ensuring that such provision is reviewed annually. Through this circular the Department for Education has taken the lead on this matter of local policy-making, and to some extent this reflects the national concern in educational circles for the future of the special needs sector in a climate of local management and delegation of services. Nevertheless, there is a national need for policy, with a common language of agreed terms, not least what constitutes special needs. The questions are, how are such policy documents to be developed, who is going to frame them, and who are the parties involved? There is a need to develop policy at the authority level, the school level and for the development of national policy documents as more schools opt out of the local authority system and become grant maintained. Whichever sector of the educational service is under policy review, there needs to be consultation, and such consultation is a matter of concern for all those with a stake in the educational system.

POLICY AT THE AUTHORITY LEVEL

There will be a need at the Local Authority level for the authority officers, advisers, members, unions, headteachers and representatives of support services to convene working groups or consultative committees to consider the issues. Such groups have been very much a feature of local authority organisation in recent years, with the need in a very short space of time for agreed policies on GCSE, TVEI, in-service, the whole dissemination of National Curriculum policy and practice, and the need for school development plans and curriculum audits. Although they may be suffering from over-consultation, local authorities certainly have the machinery and infrastructure for implementing such a policy-making progress.

As a consequence, such local authorities as far apart as Kent, Clwyd, Oldham and Nottingham already either have or are carrying out such reviews and documentation. Others, such as Manchester, Northampton, Lancashire and Kirklees, are developing their consultation procedures and drawing up policy statements in special needs. All authorities must complete a policy review by 1993.

Although such a process may appear drawn out and long-winded, the decided advantages, at least on a whole authority approach, are that all the stakeholders have been involved, there is a sense of ownership about the decisions made, and the process of dissemination can take place through the representative groups who were party to the development of the policy document itself.

In addition to this local development, as indicated earlier, a national review of special needs is long overdue; the legislation found in the Education Act 1981 which arose out of the findings of the Warnock Committee 1978 now seems somewhat remote. The Audit Commission Report *Getting in on the Act* (1992a) reveals a number of significant shortcomings in terms of statementing, appeals, and parental choice of schools. However, it could be said that there was nothing wrong with the legislation but that what has flawed the matter is the clear lack of resource allocation, as Mary Warnock recently indicated (*Guardian*, 20 October 1992), not least for the 18 per cent in mainstream schools. The momentous impact of the Education Act 1988, which seems to have considered special needs as an afterthought, poses major strategic problems. Certainly Circulars 28/89 and 7/91 attempt to redeem this matter by clearly requesting that all local authorities should develop a policy for special needs which accommodates the demands of the National Curriculum and the change to local management of schools. The Education Bill 1993 goes some way to meeting the need for a national review in this area. The development of policy documents on the part of local authorities or at least revising existing policy documents is clearly an urgent matter before local management is extended to special schools.

POLICY AT THE SCHOOL LEVEL

Individual schools, in their turn, will be required to reflect on their own policy statements as part of their development planning in these matters, and as the White Paper 1992 clearly states, grant-maintained schools will not be exempt from both providing for special needs and reflecting this in their own policy statements.

For mainstream schools there is a vested interest, indeed a survival factor, in maintaining a policy of support for the 20 per cent of children in the mainstream, if not at least to acknowledge the lobbying of 20 per cent of the parents of such children. It may be that some schools will need to formulate a joint policy, so that clusters and consortia will provide for such children in a particular catchment area. The Education Bill 1993 indicates that every school will have a

JOINT ACTION ON POLICY DEVELOPMENT

As the Children Act is comparatively new, it is difficult to predict at this time how often this provision will be used to meet the educational needs of children who are assessed under its provision. However, what this discussion illustrates and underlines is the requirement for services for children to be co-ordinated between the different providing authorities and for policy to become part of a whole authority, or whole area, or whole region, approach. In this way, Health and Social Service departments are party to policy development. In Clwyd and in many other authorities, senior and middle managers meet in joint care planning teams and joint consultative committees to share policy planning at the strategic level, so that policy changes and joint initiatives are shared and regulated. This is clearly necessary where joint assessments are made, for example under the statementing procedures, or where common provision is made such as residential schooling, or where ancillary or para-medical support is required, such as clinical or educational psychology, child guidance, speech therapy or physiotherapy. Many of the present difficulties relating to provision for children with special needs arise out of inadequate liaison between health, social services and education, with a lack of joint policy initiatives.* Over a period of 18 years involved in joint care planning in two different local authorities, the author saw very considerable liaison achieved, considerable savings made and a number of joint care initiatives achieved, not least ten years of development and co-operation for the mentally handicapped, under the All Wales Strategy.

It is imperative that policy, at least at the centre for special educational needs, clearly accommodates the statutory legislation. It is worth saying that monitoring the Education Act 1981 and the outworking is clearly to be retained by local education authorities even if most of their other responsibilities are delegated, but the responsibility of raising, maintaining and monitoring statements is expected to be held at the centre. Even if schools opt for GM status the local authority will need to carry out assessments and seek placements for children in such schools.

In developing a policy on special needs, the legislation therefore needs to be interpreted and articulated at the local level and in accordance with the values and mission of the authority and schools.

---

* Certainly the implementation of the Children Act has required close liaison on planning between all local authority departments and health authorities.

RECOGNITION OF THE CURRICULUM NEEDS

Policy documents need to take account of curriculum directives and guidelines for all children. For example, the National Curriculum Council guide-lines *From Policy to Practice* (NCC, 1988) and *A Curriculum for All* (NCC, 1989) would need to be recognised. The Education Reform Act 1988 states quite clearly that every pupil should have a broad, balanced and differentiated curriculum which promotes the spiritual, moral, cultural and mental development and prepares them for the opportunities, responsibilities and experiences of adult life. Such documents therefore encourage the development of integration and access providing a common curriculum for all children, whatever their needs.

Policy statements usually incorporate a series of objectives which are derived from the mission statement: for example, the Manchester policy document (1993) has the following objectives: 'To help mainstream schools better to meet the educational requirements of those of their pupils who experience learning difficulties which bring them under the 1981 Act.' Because integration lay at the heart of their mission, this was articulated as a policy objective in the statement that 'situations where pupils with learning difficulties attend mainstream schools should be created'.

THE RANGE OF PROVISION FOR SPECIAL NEEDS

Policy development may well go on to cover the range of provisions offered by the local authority. It should cover the whole range of transitions, from home, nursery, pre-school provision on to primary, secondary and post-school provision, with a range of provisions in between, including assessment centres, units, and special schools, both day and residential. Within this statement of provision, attention needs to be given as mentioned above to the curriculum provided and the forms of assessment used. So reference would be made to the fact that the organisation and curriculum in special schools should mirror that found in primary and secondary schools, and that assessment of children's learning will be continuous, with accurate records of attainment being kept.

It is relevant to mention that policy statements on curriculum content need to be subject to regular if not annual review. With the onset of the Education Act 1981, the policy statement developed in Clwyd reflected the curriculum requirements of the time. So the policy then developed, and referred to a tiered curriculum provision, from mainstream, mainstream with support, to a modified and then a developmental curriculum. As a consequence, when a full review was undertaken with the onset of the Education Reform Act 1988, the emphasis was on access and a common curriculum for all, with the concentration on a differentiated curriculum approach.

POLICY FOR SUPPORT SERVICES FOR SPECIAL NEEDS

A further factor in policy development is the need for clarification of support service provision. The organisation and availability of centrally provided support services has been subject to considerable rationalisation, with the onset of local management of schools and the partial effort to complete delegation of support services, an issue which will be given greater cover in the next chapter. In developing policy under the local management of schools arrangements, authorities will need to clarify which services are retained and what is their role and function and which services will be delegated to schools and how this will operate. The emphasis in the Education Reform Act 1988 on maximum delegation of resources and decision-making at a school level may sometimes conflict with the responsibility to make efficient use of resources and the carrying out of local authority statutory responsibilities. The shift of decision-making and resources to schools must therefore be matched by the retention of sufficient means to discharge statutory responsibilities and to enable other essential authority-based services to be delivered, to ensure the retention of certain specialist provision. There are clear difficulties in delegating all central services, as some authorities appear to be doing, and also in retaining specialist skills and cover for an authority's statutory responsibilities. The responsibility of having a coherent special needs policy, which is kept under review and in which the progress of individuals and the quality of provision is monitored, will require a coordinated strategy. In fact, a major requisite for support services allocation in policy formation is that a co-ordinated strategy is developed throughout an authority. The policy development in Clwyd co-ordinated all special needs support in special needs teams, working on a district basis. These teams became responsible together with schools for maintaining, monitoring and supporting special needs registers of children, which were at the heart of formula funding for special needs.

Thus any policy references to support service teams will need to consider the need for specialist assessments, the monitoring of the progress of individual pupils, support for schools in their responsibility, and to identify and assess special needs and generally act as moderation and audit agents for special needs provision within a local authority.

Assessment procedures within a special needs policy

There has been criticism in the Audit Commission Report *Getting in on the Act* (1992a) of the procedures for assessment under the

Education Act 1981 in terms of liaison with parents, the length of time taken for statements and the form and content of statements. Changes have taken place over the years, as a consequence of the Disabled Persons Act 1986, with further guidance on the review of statements and reassessments given especially for children at 14 plus. With the onset of the Education Reform Act 1988 and the requirements of the National Curriculum, Circular 22/89 gave further instruction about the form of statements in terms of curriculum assessment and provision.

The earlier Circular 3/83 provided guidelines for implementing the Education Act 1981 in terms of procedures for identification and assessment. Clwyd responded with its own interpretation of the levels of assessment leading up to section 5 statements of special needs which was then included in its policy plan.

A critical factor in all the five Warnock stages of assessment adopted by Clwyd, right up to and including the statementing procedures, was a policy based on the active involvement and participation of parents in the assessment and identification of their children, so that not only were parents' concerns listened to and acted upon but they became real partners in the process. This is clearly reiterated in the further Audit Commission Report, *Getting the Act Together* (1992b).

From the earliest stage and age in the assessment procedures, parental partnership is critical, so that in the pre-school and early school period parents can be informed and included in the assessment procedures. A guidebook for parents on this process which described their rights and highlighted the provision available throughout the school years made a significant contribution to parental co-operation and liaison in Clwyd. This was so successful that over a period of seven years from the onset of the Education Act 1981 only two appeals were made (in 1983) against the finding of a statement of special needs. As indicated earlier, the framework for assessment in Clwyd was conducted through the maintenance of special needs registers for children in schools and the development of special needs teams which included school doctors and other area health personnel. This ensured thorough regular moderation, an agreed criteria for stages of assessment and intervention county-wide. This will be considered more closely under audit in Chapter 6.

From the local authority point of view, agreed procedures, thresholds of special needs and moderation throughout the authority are needed so that a consistent and coherent arrangement across all sectors is established, so that a common language and currency is agreed.

In Chapters 6 and 8, closer attention will be paid to the criteria for thresholds of need. For the moment, a policy which includes common assessment procedures is critical to withstand provision being made on the basis of 'historical factors', or on the basis of 'need rather than greed'. Careful observations of the strengths and weaknesses of the child are vital, in both an assessment of learning and any planning for future activities. Such assessment should take account of the accessibility and relevance of the curriculum and learning experiences given to the child and such issues as school and classroom organisation and learning methods, with cultural, social, emotional and gender matters all seen as important considerations. An assessment policy will also face squarely the provision of statements of special needs, with a time factor consideration and review procedures. The starting point of such a review will be the contents of a child's statement and what has been achieved during the year, including the parents' and perhaps the child's view of this factor. The outcome of the review would list the overall objectives for the next twelve months of education for the child.

A policy for each phase of provision

For an integration policy to be developed there need to be clear guidelines for each phase of provision, as children can experience a number of transitions. Each transition should reflect the wider policy on integration and make it easy for the child and parents to move positively from one setting to another. This will happen easily where sectors have similar approaches and practices.

Provision for the under 5s/early years

This will necessarily look at children's developmental levels and requires continuous assessment of each child's learning development linked to structured record keeping. Such provision, wherever practicable, should be inclusive for all children in a given area. It may be necessary either to co-opt on to the policy making working party a pre-school co-ordinator, or better, to establish a pre-school subgroup to report back to a main committee on policy principles and practices.

School age children

With regard to school age children, as indicated earlier, the policy would reflect the wider authority policies, such as the 5–16 curriculum statements and the need for the individual schools and colleges to respond not only to these policy statements but to the requirements of the overall special needs strategy and mission.

POLICY DEVELOPMENT AT THE SCHOOL LEVEL IN THE MAINSTREAM

It would be appropriate for ease of transition and for ease of integration for schools to develop joint policies in clusters, particularly in a specific catchment area served by pre-school, primary, secondary and special schools (a point to which we will return when looking at funding and support under LMS). However, as with the under 5s, each local school should have at least a commitment to a continuous programme of assessment of children's learning requirements and curriculum development and to keep, in conformity with National Curriculum requirements, accurate records of attainment, using that information in planning, learning and sharing what they know about children's attainments with parents. Clwyd's maintenance of special needs registers ensured that accurate records were kept and such records were used to promote children's learning programmes and continuity between phases of education.

Whatever the phase or setting of the provision, mainstream or special, a broad range of curricular provision would have to be agreed by schools acknowledging the need for access and differentiation. These could provide for a mainstream curriculum provision, where the child experiences no learning difficulties, but because of their handicapping condition would need attention, given through a statement, to their specific environmental modifications. For children with mild learning difficulties, allocation to stages 1–3 of the Warnock, Clwyd or Northampton bands would be appropriate. These would require support (as we shall see in later chapters), most often through a school's special needs co-ordinator, in conjunction with class teachers, heads of department, or a teacher or therapist with specified expertise. The next group of children, those with moderate learning difficulties, would be on the threshold of statementing or statemented and would receive a more differentiated curriculum within the requirements of the National Curriculum. Such children in the mainstream should receive substantial back-up from support service teams or, if delegated, cash funding to schools based, for example, on the staffing formula of Circular 11/90, which if implemented could well achieve a common currency across all sectors in the future.

The same staffing formula could be applied to those children with severe learning difficulties where a developmental curriculum with finely graded stages and precisely defined objectives is clearly relevant. Many children in this category may well be working towards very early attainment targets at Key Stage one in some areas of the National Curriculum, yet, as *A Curriculum for All* (Fagg *et al.*, 1990) shows, can participate meaningfully in the National Curriculum.

CO-ORDINATORS FOR SPECIAL NEEDS IN MAINSTREAM SCHOOLS

There is a need for 'named persons' to be appointed in schools to carry out and oversee the implementation of integration and curriculum access programmes. The appointment of trained co-ordinators of special needs at both the primary and secondary level has gained considerable credence in educational circles. Such people are seen to be agents or facilitators of policy and practice at the school level.

As part of any short or medium plan for a whole school approach to special needs, the training of co-ordinators in both primary and secondary school is imperative. In Clwyd a programme for training co-ordinators was undertaken over the period of 1983 to 1988 on both an advanced diploma level and on a cascade model, as a prerequisite to any longer-term planning. Such a co-ordinator, with a position of responsibility in the school, particularly at middle management in a high school, is seen to be a 'key player' in the implementation of policy and good practice. They should be responsible for co-ordinating the identification and provision for special needs across a school, including advice and guidance to colleagues and consultations with parents.

Such co-ordinators, especially in secondary schools, will be members of a special needs sub-committee of the governing body, probably chaired by the governor responsible (under the Education Act 1981) for special needs, together with key managers in the school, with cross-subject representation. Such a committee will undoubtedly monitor developments and review school policy and practice. The goal of a whole school approach to special needs, in keeping with the whole authority approach, is clearly needed, with all teachers becoming skilled in teaching children with special needs by the application of a differentiated curriculum. Such approaches are often made possible by such special needs co-ordinators being instrumental in developing school policy documents and guidelines for special needs. These co-ordinators and their colleagues can prompt links in working with primary schools in the development of common screening procedures, prior to secondary school entry, to provide a smooth transition for all children, including those with special needs.

It is a task for support team personnel at secondary and particularly primary school level to work in concert with special needs co-ordinators to bring about policy change in these areas.

POLICY FOR SPECIAL SCHOOLS PROVISION

It is necessary at this stage to mention the role of the special school in policy development. Is there a future for special schools with a common curriculum and enhanced integration programmes? Many special school policy statements clearly share the view of the Warnock Report's notion of special schools being 'centres of excellence' and places where good practice and expertise can be 'exported' by outreach to the mainstream schools in its area. Authority documents on policy will need to spell out the role and future use of special schools. Policy for special schools can include support to mainstream schools on integration programmes for an increasing number of their own school populations, both part-time and full-time. I have indicated (Walters, 1993) that this may be the future for many special schools and their staff, i.e. to work with clusters of schools via support services, or as a support service in their own right, to maintain children in the mainstream and to empower mainstream teachers with new skills in inservice developments. Part of the Clwyd policy plan in the medium term was to include key special school staff to work in conjunction with special needs teams and to be nominated directly through the special needs registers for specific, specialised contributions to mainstream schools. By the time phase 1 of this policy plan was completed, some 14 special schools were supporting children and staff at various levels in over 192 mainstream schools. Of particular note was a school for children with emotional disabilities whose staff members were working almost exclusively on preventive and fixed time contracts in mainstream high schools in its local cluster. Under the LMS(S) regulations there will need to be strict service contract agreements for such arrangements, as there will be for the work of special needs teams. However, as Circular 7/91 indicates, there is certainly a clear-cut opportunity for local authorities to underwrite such outreach schemes as part of the place element for special schools.

This is already taking place, after a period of three years' development, at the Round Oak School in Warwickshire under Danks (1992), where over 50 per cent of the school staff are outreaching into a large number of primary and secondary schools. There will undoubtedly be a need for special schools to provide for some children requiring a developmental curriculum or even a modified curriculum, but experience, again in Clwyd over a number of years, shows the highly successful integration of such children across a range of primary and secondary schools. Indeed, the Ormerod School for physically handicapped children in Oxfordshire, at the last observation, although still maintaining a pre-school assessment unit, has the majority of staff working across the county supporting physically handicapped children in the mainstream, notably using conductive education techniques.

In Clwyd, as this scheme has developed and as part of its medium-to-long-term policy, a small number of special schools have closed, and staff and children have been assimilated into local primary and secondary schools and units.

As we shall consider in Chapter 6, the restructuring of special schools and the strategic planning of special school education for the rest of this century and into the next is clearly on the authority policy agenda. In the meantime, policy planning at the special school level will need regular scrutiny.

POLICY CONSULTATION AT THE AUTHORITY LEVEL

The process of policy planning and development and the need for consultation at all levels, with all the stakeholders, is a major management issue. At the local authority level the elected members, and in particular those (usually all) belonging to an education committee, are ultimately responsible to the electors in the authority for the development of policy and practice and, whilst local authorities continue in their present form, schools are accountable to the authority via the officers to the same members. However, before members of education committees receive policy statements, they are usually arrived at by a process of discussion and consultation. With respect to special needs policy making, there is need in the formulation of draft policy documents for a representative group of people to be involved in the drafting phase. There are at the local authority level, as earlier indicated, a range of joint consultative committees, joint planning teams and working parties. My experience has been that standing committees on special needs are maintained in various parts of the country covering cross-discipline and cross-agency representation and that there are a variety of special needs working parties that have developed since the onset of the Education Act 1981. These working parties were responsible, initially after Circular 3/83, for drawing up documents of guidance, standardised correspondence for parents and assessment measures, to cover education, social services and health. Guidance for parents was also often developed by such groups. These groups usually covered key persons representing schools, special and mainstream; unions; support services, especially educational psychologists; senior special needs officers, and sometimes representatives from voluntary organisations. With such representation and regular reporting back to their interest groups by the representatives, the development of policy documents can be reasonably painless. Inevitably such discussion can become protracted, especially when one interest group's needs clash with another. Compromise documents often result which can be quite bland and lacking in any significant development. To a large extent, the implementation of policy lies with the members of the authority to agree the policy and to seek a developmental framework from officers of the authority for the implementation of such policy. Any ideas for development will reflect the overall mission and values of the authority and figure in the developmental cycle which is set in an annual position statement. These position statements are set out in terms of options for implementation, and costed and presented as part of the annual cycle.

Authorities are now presenting their programmes through a business plan, usually over the lifetime of the ruling administration, which will include – if the special needs officers concerned have done their homework – a range of recommendations for implementing the special needs policy. Such developmental planning, which we will consider in subsequent chapters, is essential for progressive improvement and for realistic, i.e. within budget, targets to be set. Similarly as we shall also see later, individual schools with the extension of LMS and LMS(S) will develop their own developmental/business plans on an annual target review basis, arising out of their own policy documents.

This approach to policy development and implementation has been well-rehearsed, and if authorities are not rate-capped or forced to make large savings, they can, if they wish, carry out much of the programme set out in a special needs development plan. Some radical measures have been taken in this way and moneys provided for significant developments. Examples of note are transfer of extra-district funding for children to the development of in-county 'at home' provision by virement; the re-establishment of a special school on a mainstream (falling rolls) site, and realising the spare assets of the special school to further support the special needs programme. There are clearly many opportunities ahead under LMS(S) funding such as outreach from special schools as already mentioned, for redirection of resources and for significant policy decisions and shifts to take place.

These events can be planned for and realised where there is consensus on policy, with agreement across all levels of service provision and from all stakeholders. Where this is not the case and where such networks do not exist, then division and conflict often occurs. This is often seen where policy documents are drawn up at the centre by a professional 'caucus' usually made up of officers and, instead of detailed consultation with schools and services, brief discussion documents are issued. This approach has been the procedure followed by central government on most of the major education issues in the last two years. The pattern has been that a discussion document is issued at the end of the summer term with the closing date at the beginning of the autumn term, thereby ensuring that a minimum of consultation takes place, with minimum ownership ensuing.

However, there needs to be a balance in this process of consultation. There have been examples of long-drawn-out procedures, lasting several years, on policy documents for special needs at both the local and authority level where there have been vested interests at play or an over-zealous mood for democracy in consulting everyone. The result has been that some of those involved have fought a rearguard action on contentious issues such as school closures or service reorganisation, whilst in other cases too wide a consultation has taken so long that events overtake the process and there is a need for a further round of review before a policy can be implemented.

Clwyd, using the consultative infrastructure already in place, developed a policy document within twelve months of the onset of the Education Act 1981 in 1983 and went on to develop a review procedure in the light of the Education Reform Act 1988 some five years later, which was consulted upon and completed with a fresh policy within a further twelve months.

CONSULTATION AT THE LOCAL SCHOOL LEVEL

A local authority policy needs to be reflected at the school level, and ownership at this level needs to be real. There will be increasing problems as the local management of schools programme develops during the 1990s, whether schools reflect their local catchment needs, the felt needs of the governing body in terms of school survival or growth, or the needs of the local authority as a whole. There may well be some disagreement between individual mainstream and special schools and local authorities about the form and range of special needs provision and programmes. As a consequence, what is proposed at County Hall may not be accepted at the local school level. There is of course a requisite for all schools to implement their own development plans and audits and to state their own priorities. To a large extent these plans will need to reflect national legislation in terms of curriculum, but they may well reflect other local needs and insights rather than those of the local authority. This can work both ways in terms of special needs, and over the years there has been as much diversity in special needs provision within authorities as between them. As a consequence, many local schools in particular have developed whole school policies for special needs, appointed special needs co-ordinators at key managerial positions and opened their doors to a wide range of special needs. This has encompassed children with severe learning difficulties, as well as those with sensory deficits or physical handicaps. Conversely, others have turned their backs on special needs and become increasingly selective of their intakes and emphasised academic criteria. So in future, standard attainment target results at 11 years of age may well be the criteria for admission to some secondary schools.

At the local school level, policy documents are necessary to reflect

Action by LEAs	Action by schools	Action by both	Already in place?	Already required
LEA sets a special needs policy				
	Governors set special needs policy			
		Policy has all the essential components		
		Policy includes qualitative and quantitative indicators		
Annual report made to members				
	Annual report made to governors			
		Policy reviewed to reflect changes and indicators changed accordingly		

Figure 4.3 *Check-list for action – the special needs policy*

local needs, local interpretations and, increasingly, local aspirations. As part of the overall local authority policy document there will be a requirement for primary, secondary and special schools to produce in their school documentation development plans proposals showing how the authority special needs policy is to be implemented at their local level (see Figure 4.3 for an action check-list). Similarly, support service teams will present their policy proposals reflecting the whole authority policy at the service level. Services may well display such policy developments in their brochures as part of the marketing of their organisation to their customers. In the same way, individual schools or groups of schools will display the overall authority policy at their local level. When such local policies are developed, as part of the school development cycle, they will address such issues as staff development, curriculum differentiation, adaptation of premises, out-reach to mainstream, working in groups, or whatever the local needs demand. Clearly, such local policies will need to be co-ordinated and monitored by the local authority inspectorate and advisory services. Where special needs teams operate in these settings, they will also act as agents on behalf of both the authority and local schools by using their support network to realise the wider policy aims at the local level. For example, in key areas in Clwyd, a magnet key school was identified for integrating deaf children at the secondary level, and prime-sited schools were identified for easy adaptation for the physically handicapped. Similarly, special and residential schools had link programmes and bridging courses with mainstream schools and colleges of further education. This illustrates the need for a strategic approach, a whole authority approach and a co-ordinated team approach to the making and implementing of policy, so that economical and efficient provision is made across the system.

As stated at the beginning of this chapter, a major reason for the high priority accorded to co-ordinated policy planning is the increas-ing delegation of responsibility for management to the local level for both mainstream and special schools. For such delegation to be con-ducted efficiently and equitably agreed, policy documents need to be agreed and to be firmly in place at the local authority level.

5

Local management of schools and special needs (LMS)

The train standing at Platform Seven . . .

POLICY STATEMENTS AND LOCAL MANAGEMENT

The need for policy documents on special needs, at least at local authority level, was highlighted in Circular 7/88, section 63, when it clearly reiterated section 2(4) of the Education Act 1981 that 'LEAs are required to keep under review the arrangements made by then for special education'. It is further stated that

> the effective delivery of special education throughout an LEA depends upon a clear and coherent authority-wide policy. Such a policy must be made clear to the governing bodies and staff of the schools and the other agencies with which the LEA is required to collaborate.

The requirement for LEAs to produce policy documents is therefore now imperative. Circular 7/91, section 64, clearly states that a policy document must accompany all LEA proposals for local management schemes if they are to be extended to special schools for implementation by April 1994.

Such policies are clearly overdue, considering the fact that local management of schools was introduced in Circular 7/88 (September 1988), when considerations for special needs formulae for schools were being made. Clear policies at that stage would have overcome some of the difficulties that have been encountered in the years since 1988 on implementing special needs formulae for ordinary schools, an issue we will consider in Chapter 6.

THE ADVANTAGES OF LOCAL MANAGEMENT FOR SPECIAL NEEDS

The whole area of local management of schools raises important issues for special needs.

The development of the self-managing school is certainly an important issue in local management for special needs. By making schools responsible for all of their activities, the ideas of ownership and planning responsibility at the local level are developed within the policies of the local education authority. Local management gives greater power to individual schools to reflect their local needs and use resources to the best effect by setting their own priorities. Within these priorities, schools can develop a management flexibility in moving funds between budget headings, thus responding to local needs.

Such local management enables LEAs to be freed from local issues to develop a more strategic role of monitoring school performance and to provide professional advice and guidance to schools and governing bodies. As a consequence, it is envisaged that there will be a manpower shift from the centre to the periphery with education departments having an 'agency' style of service provision to schools. Whilst schools remain within the control of the LEAs it will be the responsibility of the LEA to establish the size of the overall budget as well as appropriate allocations to schools through clear formula funding.

THE PROBLEMS OF LOCAL MANAGEMENT FOR SPECIAL NEEDS

There are, however, also problems and risks in this area of delegating resources and responsibilities to schools. As stated earlier, LEAs still retain their statutory powers under the Education Act 1981, and the new Education Act 1993, for identification and provision for children with special needs.

As schools are delegated resources for special needs, it is intended that they begin to assume responsibility for the problems they encounter and to develop a whole school approach to such children. This leaves the authority free to adopt a monitorial role, rather than a crisis management role, of intervention. There have been problems so far in the LMS schemes prepared by LEAs for providing schools with resources under the LMS proposals. In Circular 7/88, para. 104, the Department for Education argues that the formula allocation for special needs 'must be clear, simple and predictable . . . so that governors, headteachers, parents and the community can understand how it operates and why it yields the results it does'. However, simplicity at the expense of equity is indefensible, especially where resources are scarce. One noticeable feature of this simplicity model has been the early practice of most LEAs to use the criterion of free school meals for funding special needs for non-statemented pupils. These responses have been criticised as equating special needs with social deprivation or poverty. However, authorities are required to construct objective funding allocations for special needs, and the Department for Education has been watchful of attempts to replicate historic funding. As a result many LEAs have been required in their discussions on approval of schemes for delegation, with the Department for Education, to restructure their proposals before they can be approved.

Her Majesty's Inspectorate produced a report in February 1993 on the local management of schools and pupils with special needs; in a study of 54 schools, the main findings can be seen in the following areas:

- There is a need for LEAs to develop more satisfactory indicators of the incidence of SEN. The use of free school meals, either by entitlement or actual take up, was not a wholly satisfactory indicator of the varying number of pupils with SEN in individual schools, particularly where a minimum threshold had been included for schools to receive funding in respect of pupils with SEN.

Although the use of free school meals (FMS) as a formula for funding was widespread,

- LEAs differed on the use of FSM within their formula. Some used the actual take up of FSM as the determinant of funding for SEN whereas others used entitlement to FSM, rather than take up. Schools in one LEA persuaded parents who were entitled to FSM but had not exercised this entitlement to do so on the grounds that this would increase future funding to the school. Where the take up of FSM was the determining factor, schools were disadvantaged where parents who objected to the stigma, perceived or real, of receiving FSM, or where the meals were unattractive to pupils, made alternative arrangements. (In one case, over 50 per cent of pupils had claimed FSM whilst in Year 6 of a primary school the previous year, but only 16 per cent of the same pupils were claiming FSM in Year 7 of the secondary school to which they had transferred; this had a significant effect on funding for SEN at the secondary school);
- almost all schools visited expressed a strong commitment to pupils with SEN and a determination to continue to allocate staffing and other resources to work with such pupils. There were indications that some schools were beginning to experience difficulty in achieving this, especially in LEAs where there had been reductions in the education budget. There is a need for LEAs to monitor the extent to which reductions, whether related to charge-capping or to LMS, result in less than adequate provision;
- some centrally-funded staff were developed inappropriately to work with individual pupils rather than groups, because schools

feared the removal of such staff if they were not working solely with named pupils. In such cases the LEAs should consider whether other ways of working would be more appropriate to the needs of the particular pupils and would contribute more effectively to the implementation of a whole-school policy for provision for pupils with SEN;

- the mixture of school-based and centrally-funded staff, who might be withdrawn, made it difficult for schools to plan effectively for support to pupils with SEN. This needs to be addressed within the context of LEAs' overall planning in respect of provision for pupils with SEN and in the light of changes introduced by DES Circular 7/91 and WO Circular 38/91, including the extension of local management to special schools;
- The level of provision of INSET relating to pupils with SEN having declined, there is a need in many schools for INSET about the preparation of effective teaching materials and the use of teaching styles which enable full participation in the curriculum by pupils with SEN. There is also a need for some schools to review existing practice in relation to curriculum and organisation, if pupils with SEN are to realise effectively their entitlement to a broad balanced curriculum.

Further proposals for a new framework for local management of schools were issued by the Department for Education in January 1993. These proposals set out a new national framework for the local management of schools from 1 April 1995. They redefine the term 'potential school budget' (PSB) (the amount of money capable of being delegated) and will allow schools to control much of their own budget.

The proposals include the following:

- increasing the level of PSB delegation (from 1 April 1993, LEAs will be required to delegate of the 85 per cent of the PSB to schools. It is proposed that this should rise to 90 per cent of the redefined PSB from 1 April 1995 to April 1996 for Inner London);
- a requirement that LEAs should in future hold back money relating to education psychology and welfare services, and the budget for premature retirement and dismissal costs;
- allowing all special schools to receive fully delegated management powers over their budgets from 1 April 1996;
- placing special units for pupils with SEN, which are part of mainstream schools, under the management of their host schools rather than the LEA from 1 April 1995;
- suggestions for relaxing formula funding rules for pupils with statements of SEN placed individually or in small groups in mainstream schools;

• retaining the present policy of requiring schools to be charged actual salary costs.

TO STATEMENT OR NOT TO STATEMENT?

One of the major difficulties with delegation of resources to schools for special needs has been the differences between provision for statemented and non-statemented pupils, especially where statements have been seen to be a discretionary exception. With differing thresholds between authorities and no clear criteria within many authorities for statementing, there has been a marked increase in the number of requests for statementing of children. This is clearly the problem highlighted by Coopers & Lybrand in 1988. If a high level of resources is allocated for statemented pupils there may be a tendency for schools to be too hasty to seek a classification of need at the statementing level in order to maximise their overall level of resources. This significant increase in requests for statements has varied, for example, in the 18 months to September 1990 with a 56 per cent increase in Sheffield and in the 12 months to September 1990 a 40 per cent rise in Rotherham (Pyke, 1990). These figures are clearly paralleled in many parts of the country.

Nevertheless, where there is a clear strategy and criteria for levels of intervention for special needs including a criteria for statementing, then statementing requests can be brought under control. In Clwyd, where special needs registers are maintained, the requests for statementing are managed by close area monitoring by special needs support teams and school special needs co-ordinators. Although there was some increase in statementing requests, when these registers were used for formula funding under LMS, it has now 'levelled off' (Audit Commission, 1992b).

This issue clearly concerns the Select Committee enquiring into the statementing of children with special needs. Amongst the questions they are asking and seeking evidence about are:

(i) At what level of special educational need should children be 'statemented'?
(ii) What are the main reasons for the wide variation in the proportion of children with statements in different LEAs?

The first question could be answered by the use of registers of need based on the Warnock five levels of need, with intervention at level 5 being the statementing threshold. The second question clearly raises issues of the historical development of provision for special needs in differing LEAs, both at the mainstream and special schools levels. Some authorities have very well developed in-school provision with whole school policies towards special needs. As a consequence, their 'threshold' for 'triggering off' statements is contingent on these factors.

THE NEED FOR A COMMON FORMULA FUNDING

As the Select Committee questions show, LEAs are extremely varied in their approaches to formula funding under LMS. National Curriculum tests are being used in some authorities; others, like Clwyd, are using composite indices of need. In fact the Clwyd model of special registers as quoted in Audit Commission (1992), can be taken further by using the numbers on the school register and adding factors, such as size of school, whether rural or urban and socio-economic factors, which might include free school meals. Other factors could be added including unemployment statistics, or even ethnic minority groupings (although this is not necessarily a special education factor as laid down in the Education Act 1981).

Such indices could be weighted against educational, economic, social or school factors and a formula provision applied to each school. On this basis for example, there may be a need to positively discriminate towards small rural schools or a school in poor premises in an urban area. Such a formula, once agreed, would apply to all provision given to schools both under LMS procedures and also for added support and time allocation for educational psychologists, educational social workers, ancillary support, and specialist advisory support. The following descriptions of this process shows how this can be arrived at.

The factors

The number on roll and the number of children in each of the categories deemed important to the calculation of the LMS allocation for each school are entered on to a large spreadsheet. These categories are the factors then used by the system to calculate the final outcome for each school.

The ratio measures

It is of interest to compare each of the factors used to arrive at the final allocation to the total number on roll at any one school. This ratio will automatically take into account such factors as school size. Given that rural schools, for example, may tend to be smaller than those in an urban setting, an element of bias may thus be introduced to favour such schools.

The weightings

Weightings are applied to the factors deemed to be of interest. If these factors are assigned a value between 0 and 1 and the sum over all the factors to be equal to one, i.e. the factors are normalised, then the control of the weight of each factor is simplified. Any factor given a weighting of 0 (zero) will be effectively eliminated from the calculation. In this way, factors that are perceived to be of importance but not as yet quantifiable may be added to the system for reporting purposes only – e.g. various socio-economic factors may be identified as important – yet be difficult, if not impossible, to quantify at the moment. By entering them into the system, their significance has been noted, and this fact would then be included in any report produced.

The weightings for the various factors are held on a separate spreadsheet and this small spreadsheet is used to control the behaviour of the system as a whole. This means that any changes may easily be made and the result of such changes will be rapidly calculated and reported, thus enabling the professionals involved to evaluate the validity of the model.

It may be useful to split the factors into three sub-groups:

(1) level of statement (stages 1 to 5);
(2) socio-economic indicators;
(3) school indicators (size or setting indicators)

Each of this sub-groups may be given special consideration – e.g. group (1) might be given a combined weighting of 0.6 (60 per cent) and the other two groups share the remaining 0.4 weighting between them. The only restriction is that the combined sum of all the weightings should equal 1.

Relative weighting of the groupings could encourage schools to use, for example, in-school resources and retain children at stages 2 or 3. Table 5.1 shows the index outline.

DEFINITIONS OF LEVELS OF NEEDS

As indicated in Chapter 2, the whole area of definition of needs, whether educational or social, requires clarification before indices are set. Definitions of need can influence indicators and the use of too many indicators may have a detrimental effect, e.g. a test producing low scores produces more money and rewards poor schools. So different LEAs have responded in different ways to the needs–resources ratio (see Figure 5.1).

Table 5.1 *Downtown School Anywhere in Clwyd: special needs index*

Primary special needs register numbers	Statements variable type	Socio-economic unemployment, etc. weighted	Socio-economic, free school meals	Urban/very, very rural	School size
Stage I	Mild				Very small
Stage 2	Moderate Severe				Small Middle
Stage 3	PH Sensory				Large
Stage 4	EBD				Very large

Totals: $\times \frac{100}{6} = £$ formula for the school index applies to all areas of special needs provision

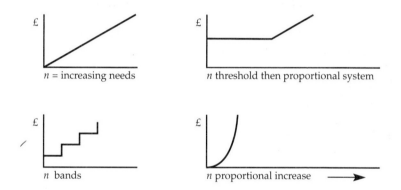

Figure 5.1 *How different LEAs have responded to the needs resources ratio. However, the problem still exists in weighting appropriate priorities*

SPECIAL NEEDS INDICES OF NEED

Lee (1992) shows that there is a considerable range of other factors for allocating special needs resources under LMS in England and Wales and a wide range of funding thresholds. A pupil with special needs may attract an extra £390 in a Cambridgeshire school's budget, whilst the same pupil might expect around £11 in Durham.

Lee further shows that there are authorities using the LMS formula for funding statemented pupils in special units in mainstream schools with a range of funding from £6,185 for profound and multiple hearing difficulties to £2,033 for other learning difficulties. This could be seen as a forerunner of LMS(S) funding formulae for special schools.

The Kent special needs audit and the Northampton audit both tackle this problem head-on by providing a common formula across all sectors with the concept of special needs age-weighted pupil units. This does of course reduce children's needs to units of need and, as seen in the categories also allocated in Cumbria, returns to some extent to a form of categorisation found in the pre-Warnock era.

LMS AND THE ROLE OF SUPPORT SERVICES

Another major issue raised by the Select Committee's 1992 question-naire in the field of delegation is that of delegation or non-delegation of support services. Should LEAs retain centrally-funded support services for children with special needs? Support services are a budget area within the discretionary exceptions available to LEAs to be retained at the centre. However, this area is no more than 10 per cent of the general schools budget, and with the development of the potential schools budget by 1 April 1993 (1995 for inner London LEAs) there will be delegation of at least 85 per cent of the PSB by this date. Already, therefore, support services, although discretionary exceptions, have increasingly become part of the delegation process. Some authorities are proposing to delegate all support service budgets to schools. From the Lunt and Evans review (1992, p. 27), 15 LEAs reported that changes were planned for such services and ten said they were under review.

The Special Educational Needs Advisory Council (Gomer *et al.*, 1990) survey of LEAs in England and Wales revealed that support services seemed to have the sole responsibility for facilitating the movement of children into integrated mainstream settings (although special schools outreach work was also a contributory factor). In their survey, 44 per cent of the authorities consulted indicated no change of role for their support services; whilst 7 per cent indicated making changes. This included reorganising and retaining some services centrally for monitoring LMS special needs provision and monitoring registers, and just two authorities decentralising and delegating services to schools.

One of the problems revealed by this survey of support service provision is that there is a variety of provision of varying quality for special needs across the country. Thus whilst 96 per cent of the authorities in the SENNAC survey provided support for sensory deficit, only 16 per cent provided for children with specific learning difficulties.

It is certain that, whatever ratios or formulae for SENs are devised nationally or locally, there is going to be a need for close monitoring and quality control. So in response to the Select Committee question put earlier on delegation of support services or central control, there are major issues to consider. There is an overwhelming need to monitor the effectiveness and efficiency of provision of special needs resources if LEAs are to carry out their responsibilities under the Education Act 1981. Support service teams are well-qualified to undertake this moderation. This cannot be left to the OFSTED four-year inspection cycle when allocation of service resources are necessary through an annual audit. Continued specialist support of psychologists, social workers and special needs support personnel could be allocated on a strategic basis, where they are shared between both mainstream and special schools.

THE ARGUMENT FOR LEAs RETAINING MANAGEMENT OF SUPPORT SERVICES

It could be argued that during the last decade a considerable wealth of expertise has been developed by LEAs which could be lost if support services are delegated. Further, the continuous training and development of such teachers and other professionals can only be undertaken on a strategic management basis. There is already a shortfall in training places funded by LEAs for educational psychologists. If authorities are finding it difficult to fund training at the strategic level, what chance would schools have of effecting such training opportunities?

Amongst the other issues on the delegation of support services under LMS procedures is the problem of how the LEA can ensure that the resources delegated for SEN pupils will be used for this purpose by the schools concerned. Anyone dealing at the sharp end of crisis management in an ordinary school will agree that when staff are away, when priorities are being tabled, as competition between schools begins to take effect, then something has to give, and often the most vulnerable area is special needs provision, particularly in small schools. There is a valid role here for support services to ensure that the LEA special needs provision and policies are appropriately monitored. Support service networks, particularly of the integrated kind, incorporating psychological services, sensory deficit services, behavioural support services and support for a variety of integrated statemented children, provides a valuable resource for any local authority, particularly where they work together in supporting clusters of schools. Such developments at the local level in authorities such as Oldham, Clwyd, Kent and Northampton have been made in the light of some of the far-sighted recommendations of the Fish Report (1985), which proposed an integrated support service for special needs which met the needs of pupils wherever they were taught. Where reviews of policy and provision have taken place in recent years, they have generally favoured the retention of centrally-held services for the reasons stated above. This has been particularly evident in Cheshire and Northampton.

INCREASING DELEGATION AND COMPETITION

However, it is becoming clearer that as LEAs are moving towards the maximum delegation of funds intended by Circular 7/91, greater pressure will be made upon centrally held services to be delegated. Indeed, some are already moving towards an agency model for all centrally held services, not least inspectors and advisers, and through such agencies offering service agreements to schools to enable them to buy in such service time and expertise out of delegated moneys. As the OFSTED training package is being offered to people outside the LEAs the 'market' may present other providers of services besides those held centrally by LEAs, whether on an agency basis or other-wise. As more schools opt out of LEAs and become grant-maintained, and as the 1993 Act provides for alternative funding of schools through a central funding agency at the 10 per cent level to the 75 per cent level of joint funding, so then could LEAs be said 'not to exist' with regard to funding schools. There are already, in some authorities, education mergers with social services departments, combining forces to fulfil their joint responsibilities under the Children Act and Education Act 1993.

The need for LEAs to develop service agreements and policy guidelines for support services to schools, as mentioned in Chapter 4, is an urgent task before enhanced delegation forces the issue.

DEVELOPING SERVICE CONTRACTS UNDER LOCAL MANAGEMENT

The psychological service in Clwyd undertook a review of its service to schools in 1990 and consequently developed a policy for support, including a service agreement with schools which included contract times and quality controls.

Northampton intends to retain as centrally funded only those services which fulfil statutory or essential specialist functions and expects to delegate the funding for all non-specialist tasks and those roles and functions which are best managed by schools, so that they can exercise maximum choice over the level or type of support required. As a consequence, service agreements are being drawn up for these essential specialist tasks so that the authority can have a responsive system which reflects schools needs. Service contracts are intended to include the following criteria to:

- reflect the client's needs;
- define manageable tasks with clear boundaries;
- identify and apportion responsibilities;
- establish a time frame and set up reporting relationships;
- define charges where appropriate;
- involve all relevant personnel;
- make provision for evaluating results.

The role of the support service in Northampton is to be closely linked to the functions of other special education provision so that a continuum of provision is made. Similarly, service agreements can also be made with education welfare support and curricular advisory teams. There is a real danger, if such inter-service arrangements are not closely linked, of an atomisation of support services within an authority, each forming their own service agreements and being in direct competition with one another. Schools may well, in reduced budgeting circumstances, take on the cheapest service contract available.

The pressures for enlarged delegation demonstrated in the White Paper and enshrined in the Education Act 1993 have persuaded many LEAs to produce similar schemes to that of Northampton. Thus Clwyd and Cheshire have set up a central core team of special needs personnel to undertake statutory duties. In Clwyd's case this is to monitor levels of need and the structure of special needs through school-based registers. Other statutory duties such as identification, assessment and review under the 1981 Act and the provision of specialist teaching and support for statemented pupils, e.g. dyslexia, hearing and visual impairments, will also be monitored. The budget for the remainder has been delegated to schools on the basis of the special needs register support identified. The experience to date is that schools overall have remained 'loyal' to the special needs policy, and in fact in a significant number of cases 'bought in' more specialist support out of their own resources. Fears therefore in this direction of diluted support are so far unfounded.

A similar pattern has been developed in Cheshire, where proposals for a core team to be held centrally are well in hand, again to carry out statutory responsibilities in the six areas of the county on a multi-disciplinary basis. These core teams will manage and monitor the 'fast track' agency provision of support to schools of SEN pupils identified through SEN registers. Thus funds will be delegated to schools, who will 'buy in' from the agency a range of support for the school as a whole and for individual pupils through service level agreements. The support personnel will also transfer appropriate special needs data back to the care team. Coopers & Lybrand (1992) suggest that specialist services to schools such as learning support for pupils with special educational needs may well be organised across a number of schools to make them viable. As such, they usually require a minimum number of schools to make a commitment to their use. Where service agreements are not practical for very small clusters, there has been a reluctance by a number of LEAs to delegate funding for these services to protect the interests of the majority of schools. Where funds are delegated, schools may find that they are offered a sliding scale of charges for these services, depending on the number of schools signing up to use, and hence fund them. This will need a collective decision by schools on whether they wish the service to be available or not. Alternative providers of such services are largely restricted to trained in-school staff, or it may be individuals outside the formal LEA service, who are willing to provide a service on an *ad hoc* basis.

With regard to educational psychology services and educational welfare, Coopers & Lybrand (1989) have indicated that some part of these services, such as inservice on offering advice to schools about ways of integrating pupils with special needs in mainstream, could be delegated. Schools are then free to buy back the service they require. Again, alternative providers could be found in other LEAs (if they are permitted to cross county boundaries), specialist consultancies and higher education institutes.

Coopers & Lybrand (1989) further indicate that schools may wish to buy in extra support for educational psychologists, for example to supplement their existing provision. However, LEAs may be reluctant to make such provision available if the aim of the school is to exert more pressure for statementing of pupils and hence more resources, rather than to make in-school provision. A further dimension to these arrangements is that the agency provision can also draw up service level agreements with the LEA who, under the enhanced delegation proposals, would buy back 80 per cent of all service provision (see Figure 5.2).

THE ADVANTAGES OF SERVICE CONTRACTS

The Audit Commission (1992b, p. 52) regards service contracts as having several virtues. These are as follows:

- it assists the LEA in its monitoring role;
- it provides a means of allocating funding to non-statemented

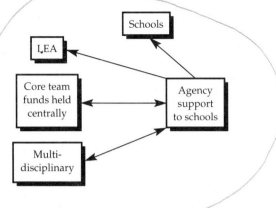

Figure 5.2 *Agency service level arrangements*

SEN pupils on an equitable consistent basis, targeting identified needs;
- it raises awareness of SEN issues through discussions which take place on school visits;
- such agreements will ensure appropriate and consistent systems of identification, assessment and review of pupils under the Education Act 1981 procedures·

Arising from this, some schools have already indicated requests for enhanced special needs visit provision from, for example, the core team in Cheshire.

This strategy co-ordinates and implements the county's SEN policy through the management role of the core team via the learning support service agency through the following:

- consistent practice and record keeping;
- professional development;
- staff appraisal;
- appropriate allocation of staff in terms of experience, skills and expertise related to pupils' special educational needs. This 'correct fit' is essential to retain service credibility and effective provision for the diverse special needs population.

The core team and senior managers using this model in both Clwyd and Cheshire are able to monitor and evaluate the annual cycle of the special needs support service in order to ensure quality provision through appropriate performance indicators.

Overall, early indications in these authorities suggest a buy-back of 80 per cent with only a modest degree of change and only a 10 per cent risk. There is a need with schemes of this kind 'to get close to

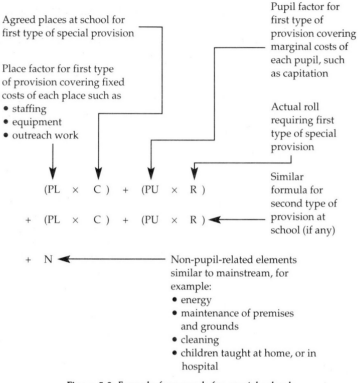

Agreed places at school for first type of special provision

Place factor for first type of provision covering fixed costs of each place such as
- staffing
- equipment
- outreach work

Pupil factor for first type of provision covering marginal costs of each pupil, such as capitation

Actual roll requiring first type of special provision

$$(PL \times C) + (PU \times R)$$

$$+ (PL \times C) + (PU \times R)$$

Similar formula for second type of provision at school (if any)

$$+ N$$

Non-pupil-related elements similar to mainstream, for example:
- energy
- maintenance of premises and grounds
- cleaning
- children taught at home, or in hospital

Figure 5.3 *Formula framework for special schools*

Source: NUT (1990), p. 35

the customer' to ascertain the client's needs and to prepare a marketing plan, a subject to which we will return in a later chapter. Further it is quite clear that in order for schemes of this kind to work, a 'tight', agreed, well-moderated audit of needs is managed on an annual basis, with agreed criteria for levels of need and support. This issue has been closely addressed by other authorities, particularly Kent and Northampton, and will be discussed in Chapter 6. There are of course concerns about security of contracts for staff on a medium-term basis and the problem of replacing staff on short-term contracts for this kind of agency work.

LOCAL MANAGEMENT AND SPECIAL SCHOOLS

The final link in the chain of local management of schools is the local management of special schools LMS(S) to be introduced by April 1994, with many pilot schemes already under review.

The feasibility study for extending local management to special schools undertaken by Touche Ross Management Consultants (1991) highlighted the general benefits of delegation and recommended a formula framework (see Figure 5.3 for a formula framework for special schools). The report concluded that delegation was both feasible and desirable. It recommended a system that funded according to a combination of the number and nature of the places in the special schools maintained by the LEA. The report was confident that such a system could work, and that it could work to the benefit of pupils in special schools.

In October 1990 the then Secretary of State, John MacGregor, speaking at a Spastics Society Conference, welcomed the Touche Ross report and indicated that the process of consultation on this issue would be undertaken with a view to making a decision in 1991. Circular 7/91 issued in April 1991 in section C embraced most of the recommendations found in the Touche Ross report and in section 68 stated that regulations would be issued requiring all LEAs to extend formula funding to special schools from April 1994. As a consequence, LEAs are in the process of submitting their draft schemes on LMS(S) together with their policy documents, at the latest by 30 September 1993.

In the interim period enabling regulations have persuaded many LEAs to pilot the introduction of LMS(S) to selected special schools to gain experience on the varying forms it might take. Those LEAs who wish to extend LMS to special schools earlier must submit their proposals at least six months before they are due to come into force. In the meantime, the Department of Education has produced Circular 11/90 on staffing for special needs which for the first time since 1975 provided a formula for special needs staffing across a general band of needs in terms of teacher time and special (SSA) assistant time per child (see Table 5.2). For some authorities this provided a common if rather crude language of indices of support for special needs in both mainstream and special schools as well as a useful platform on which to develop LMS(S) formulae whilst they were also experimenting with

Table 5.2 *Staffing level formula for special needs*

Band of learning difficulty	Primary		Secondary	
	Teacher	SSA	Teacher	SSA
Profound and multiple learning difficulties	0.2	0.3*	0.2	0.3*
Severe communication difficulties	0.18	0.18	0.18	0.18
Severe emotional and behavioural difficulties	0.15	0.15	0.15	0.15
Severe developmental difficulties	0.13	0.13	0.13	0.13
Other learning difficulties	0.1	0.1	0.1	0.05

*In a group of ten pupils the maximum number of SSAs will be three.

LMS special needs formulae. This became a key issue for some authorities, such as Kent, who believed that the staffing formula for special needs should be the same for all sectors, mainstream, units and special schools.

In a letter to all chief education officers in England and Wales (Clark, 1993), the Department for Education outlined some major factors that authorities needed to consider before extending LMS to special schools. These included the following points on formula funding:

- does the scheme variation provide for all the authority's special schools to be funded by formula from the start of the variation scheme?
- is the authority proposing a combination of predominantly place-led funding with some pupil-led funding (i.e. 'the Touche Ross model')?
- if funding is to be predominantly place-led, is it clear:
  (1) what proportion (roughly) of the ASB is to be allocated by (a) place factors; (b) pupil factors?
  (2) is there a statement of the authority's intentions regarding future reviews of the number of planned places?
  (3) is there a schedule listing the different place factors with brief descriptions of the provision to which the place factor relates?
  (4) are the definitions clearly stated?
- are the proposed arrangements for funding special schools compatible with the special schools' formal terms of approval ('recognised accommodations') in respect of overall capacity, age range and type of provision (e.g. EBD, MLD, etc.)?
- do the arrangements for place and/or pupil funding contain any weightings for age, and if so are they clearly stated?
- are the arrangements for funding any residential special schools specified?
- are residential schools to be funded via an enhanced place factor?
- are there proposals to fund hospital schools? If so, are they clearly set out and in line with the advice contained in paragraph 73 of Circular 7/91?
- does the variation scheme contain any proposals to fund special schools for outreach work? If so:
  (1) is outreach funding delivered via enhanced place-led funding?
  (2) is this specified in the schedule listing the place elements in the scheme? Is the specification sufficiently detailed to make clear to participating schools the nature and extent of the outreach work that they will be expected to undertake?
  (3) are there conditions placed on governing bodies to ensure that participating schools play their part in outreach work?
- are the arrangements for the pupil count specified and clear?

- does the variation scheme include a small schools salary protection factor for special schools? If so:
  (1) is it clearly defined?
  (2) do the salary protection proposals include non-teaching staff and if so are the proposals clearly defined?
- does the variation scheme propose any curriculum protection factor or block allocation for special schools? If so, are the proposals clearly defined?

These questions indicate that there is some considerable planning to be done in this area by local authorities.

THE ISSUES ARISING FROM LMS FOR SPECIAL SCHOOLS

There are problems in the making for LMS(S), particularly if special schools, as in the mainstream, go into LMS(S) on a competitive basis, either against each other or other forms of special provision particularly in the mainstream. There could be a drift to special schools away from integration programmes if there is not common funding across the system.

As Circular 7/91 (section 75) clearly states, section 38(i) of the Education Reform Act 1988 requires the budget share of each school covered by the LEA scheme to be determined by the application of a formula. As far as LMS(S) is concerned, Circular 7/91 requires that an element per planned place of a defined type at each school, plus an element per pupil actually on roll, should be included. It is also open to LEAs to include other factors such as premises-related costs and costs related to exceptional needs where they form a valid basis for allocating funds to special schools. Such a case may be those occasions when an individual pupil's needs are so unusual that special provision has to be made; for example, in Clwyd a child with little or no immunity to sunlight needed very special provision and support to be made. A further element clearly available to LEAs is the work of outreach which is a distinctive feature of many special schools. I have mentioned (Walters, 1993) that such outreach work was a major feature of Clwyd's special needs policy, with 14 special schools outreaching some 132 mainstream schools on integration programmes. Before delegated budgets take a firm hold it is opportune that we examine the possibility of special schools outreach provision. If such opportunities are not taken up to promote integration, then a reverse drift will take place from a scarce, under-resourced, mainstream, closely costed provision, to the more loosely costed, still flexible provision of place element found in special schools and units.

A PILOT PROJECT UNDER LMS(S)

Clwyd piloted an LMS(S) scheme from September 1991 to March 1993 in three different types of special schools. These were an all-age day-school for children with moderate learning difficulties, a primary special needs assessment centre, and a residential all-age school for children with autistic difficulties.

In each case, the school identified received a formula-funded budget based firstly on a place element, the value assigned to each place factor reflecting the cost of teaching and non-teaching staff and specialist equipment needed to occupy the place. In the case of the residential school the cost of 24-hour care was reflected in that place factor. A consistent and common level of funding is provided for such common place factors. In this pilot the LEA determined the types and numbers of places available annually at each school. This is a critical factor in development planning, as we will see in Chapter 6. The place level is set to accommodate a stable resource base and allow for admission of pupils throughout the year.

So staffing at all levels is provided on this place formula for each school. Some LEAs have based the teacher requirement for each pupil type on the basis of Circular 11/90 staffing recommendations. The next factor is the pupil element: as each pupil is occupied at a school, an additional cost is generated. This should cover consumable items (in a residential school this is considerable) and also where pupil-related costs are high for special cases. Under this item Clwyd included in their pilot the outreach element in terms of pupils supported in mainstream schools. As this develops, a controlled programme of integrated support is maintained, especially where it is regulated within the special needs register system monitored in the mainstream schools. In Warwickshire at Round Oak School (Danks, 1992), outreach support from a special school to a range of mainstream schools in its cluster can be successfully negotiated. Opened in 1989, the school established close links with eight schools and over 50 other sites in the area, and totally integrated 45 per cent of its pupils. There are major issues of course for staff development, both at the special and mainstream level, and the need to discontinue outreach when successful levels of integration have been achieved.

It is possible under this scheme to enhance the budget share of mainstream schools so that they can reciprocate by providing mainstream staff for special schools to provide wider cover under the National Curriculum.

The final element in the formula was the premises element, where specific weighting was given to some premises needs, particularly for schools with nursery or residential facilities. However, such allocations were made not on the basis of historical costs but on the characteristics of the school premises and grounds.

INTEGRATED LMS AND LMS(S) SCHEMES

Northampton has gone some way towards developing common procedures for special needs in both mainstream and special schools based on one integrated LMS(S) and LMS scheme and using the principle that the same age and special needs attracts the same funding whenever it is found. To this end they have developed a special needs age-weighted pupil unit so that age weighting × special needs weighting × pupil type weighting = total weighting required. The levels of funding are based on the descriptions of educational arrangements to meet particular special needs. The concept of place funding for special schools will also apply to designated special provision in mainstream.

Overall, in their five-year development plan Northampton have determined the number of places to be funded, in which locations they will be found, and for which of the six bands of their special needs they will be funded. These factors will be subject to an annual audit review.

FURTHER ISSUES FOR SPECIAL NEEDS UNDER LMS

LMS and LMS(S) developments raise a number of crucial issues for special needs management. It is essential that there is an agreed formula for special needs funding across all sectors, with a common currency for staffing and clear criteria of levels of need and thresholds for statementing. As mentioned earlier, there are increasing demands for children to be statemented to provide extra resources. Some schools may well reject children who are not protected by a statement.

With regard to delegation of support services under LMS, whether whole or in part, there are dangers of the dissipation of scarce resources and expertise, with little control left at the centre for monitoring and quality control of special needs provision.

Looking at LMS(S) developments there are both threats and opportunities. This is a wonderful time for review and reorganisation of provision in special education. Many authorities are grasping the opportunity in their policy review documents. Further, this is a critical time for considering outreach support from special schools under the place element, to retain some staff and standardise outreach procedures through such systems as a special needs register. The varying types of outreach currently on offer, even within authorities, need to conform to appropriate staffing criteria and be consistent across all facilities. This is therefore an opportune time to co-ordinate such outreach support as part of an integrated support service system.

The threats are that retrenchment can set in, with special schools becoming more independent and having less contact with the mainstream, whilst mainstream schools unload their troublesome children on to the special school sector. Policy documents from LEAs are necessary to accompany proposals for LMS(S) developments before 1994. Such documents will require comprehensive development proposals for authority and school planning and contain clear audits of need so that a common currency of provision and allocation can be provided for schools and children on an equitable basis, wherever they are found. The making of such development plans and audits are discussed in Chapter 6.

Many readers may feel that the LMS programme reminds them of a railway system which is also being prepared for local management or privatisation. There was, in the days of local railway management, the old London, Midland and Scottish system (LMS) to which this poem is in part tribute with apologies to W.H. Auden.

The Era Express

This is the nightmare bringing the orders
Out of the capital, up to the borders;
Orders for governors, orders for heads,
Making them turn in their uneasy beds,
Worrying little ones still in their prime,
And teachers who cannot deliver on time,
Covering desk tops with binders and folders,
Weighing them down like enormous grey boulders,
Whistling through dreams like a demon that rages,
Hurtling along on its iron key stages.

This is the nightmare slowly ascending,
Mountains of paperwork, tests never ending,
Ranks of advisers all on the offensive
From nursery corner to state comprehensive,
Throwing out history books, tearing up parchments,
Re-educating the heads of departments,
Casting a searchlight on matters curricular,
Auditing every classroom particular.
Hurtling through concepts regardless of stress,
Racing to get there before LMS,
Puffing and straining at terrible pace,
Sweating to put all the targets in place,
Until it arrives at its last destination,
The terminal scrapyard of state education.

Out of the capital, over the borders,
This is the nightmare bringing the orders,
The cold steel of audit, assessment and test,
Laying democracy surely to rest.

6

Planning for development

Out of little acorns big oak trees grow.

THE ANNUAL PLANNING CYCLE

> The courage and imagination with which the development plan is
> drawn, the energy and judgement with which it is carried into effect,
> will not only determine the future of our educational system but may
> largely shape the future course of the nation's way forward.
> (*The Nation's Schools* (Ministry of Education, 1945))

The concept of a development plan is a familiar one at the local
authority level. All departments in local government go through the
planning and developmental cycle annually. This is subject to budget
constraints and is usually accompanied by a position statement and
a range of options. This has been the pattern over recent years, and
although local management of schools is increasingly shifting resources
and responsibility from the centre, education departments are still
responsible for budgetary controls and allocation of resources. Special
needs planning and provision is part of this development cycle.

Within this strategic planning exercise, it is clear that there is a
need for an annual audit at the centre, of both resources available
and the number of children requiring those resources, so that budget
targets can be set. To this end therefore, as policy documents are
being reviewed, so are resources and services, so that a comprehensive
audit of provision in every form can be undertaken. The concept of
formula funding explored under local management of schools is part
of this review. Similarly, so that resources available can be matched
to need, an audit of each school's need is necessary in order to clarify
the extent and range of need in that authority's schools. All this is
undertaken so that a local authority can continue to maintain its
responsibility and policy for special needs, but equally, so that it can
delegate equitably those resources available to meet special needs
which have been identified at the school level.

Similarly, at the school level the development cycle is also

Figure 6.1 *Development planning cycle*

operative. This too needs to be initiated by asking the question, where are we now in terms of provision of special needs across a range of issues and parameters?

For this process to take place however, agreed indicators of provision and indices of special need must be in place between schools if equitable decisions are to be made within authorities. This is a major task for education authorities and schools to engage in over the next few years.

The task of this chapter is to look at good practice in this field in terms of audit, development planning and monitoring and to indicate some criteria that can be used at both the authority and school levels.

There are useful guidelines for audit procedures under developmental planning for schools issued by the School Curriculum Development Committee entitled *Guidelines for Review and Internal Development in Schools* (GRIDS) for both primary and secondary level, and DES booklets on *Planning for School Development* under the auspices of the School Development Plan Project (Hargreaves, 1989; DES, 1989a). The major concern in these pages however is to concentrate on the special needs elements in these audit and planning procedures.

THE STEPS IN DEVELOPMENT PLANNING

There are various stages in development planning, the first being an audit or review of provision at whatever level. Next is the construction of the development plan with aims and objectives for development in the short, medium and long term. These objectives are then turned into specific targets which are written in terms of performance indicators. The indicators of performance are evaluated at the end of the period before the cycle of audit begins again (see Figure 6.1). In view of the controversial nature of performance indicators in the special needs field, it is proposed to leave any major discussion on this issue until Chapter 7.

ONE LOCAL EDUCATION AUTHORITY'S DEVELOPMENT PLAN FOR SPECIAL NEEDS

In Clwyd, the education development plan for 1990 included the annual analysis of all those elements of service provision for the education of children with special needs. Further, it identified the main areas where increased provision was required and then ascertained at what levels such provision would be made.

From this annual review, options were targeted and budgets set for the following year. The following aims, objectives and selection of targets indicate elements from the development plan for that year.

Education Committee aims

- to provide resources for the teaching situation and the curriculum on the basis of actual needs, not historical practice;
- to ensure the continued integration of pupils with special educational needs into mainstream schools in all cases where this is appropriate.

Policy objectives

- to provide levels of teaching and diagnostic support to ensure that pupils identified as having special educational needs in mainstream schools have the same entitlement of resources as pupils in special educational needs schools and units;
- to provide delegation of an LMS formula funding for children at stages 2–4 (special educational needs) and stage 5 (statemented pupils);
- to continue to provide facilities in specialist schools and units for certain children with special needs on a cost-effective basis, and to allocate adequate resources to enable special educational needs schools to implement the National Curriculum to the widest possible degree and to enable structured integration of pupils into mainstream setting;
- to continue to balance the use of in-county and out-of-county facilities so as to provide the most cost-effective service to pupils and to use in-county facilities whenever appropriate;
- to continue to develop in-county resources, making such placements available on occasions to other authorities;
- to develop resources and placements for children with special educational needs in both the pre-school and the tertiary sectors;

- to allocate an adequate school psychological service input on an entitlement basis arising from measurement of need, as opposed to an historical basis;
- to allocate appropriate school psychological service input to work with pre-school and post-school handicapped children and their families;
- to plan, initiate and evaluate an 'open door' community facility by which the general public can meet members of the school psychological service to receive confidential guidance regarding children without formal referral from another source;
- to develop tertiary facilities to enable access and education for all Clwyd's SEN pupils;
- to promote an increased input to professional development.

Targets

- to provide resources under LMS procedures in both primary and secondary for the special needs population both on statements of needs and on special needs registers. The potential is for 4 per cent of the school population to need statementing; the present level catered for is approximately 2.5 per cent.
- to develop the advisory teacher service to support and monitor special needs support provision for the National Curriculum in mainstream schools and to provide statementing facilities;
- to develop diagnostic support service to support special needs integration and programmes under the National Curriculum;
- to provide a diagnostic support and assessment ratio of 1 to 4,500 in pre-school and further education facilities for children and young people with special needs;
- to develop a support service for EFL (English as Foreign Language) children and for 'traveller' children to meet government guidelines. This will be linked to a grant-aided initiative from the government;
- to develop primary units provision for emotional, behavioural problem children;
- to provide the teaching and ancillary staff complement in all the county's SEN schools to facilitate the widest implementation of the National Curriculum and government guidelines;
- to provide the teaching and ancillary staff complement in all the county's SEN schools to facilitate outreach and structured integration;
- to develop the NNEB complement in all the county's SEN schools to support teaching staff and obtain best use of resources;
- to review and develop the provision for early years assessment in all areas of the county;
- to provide appropriate facilities and resources to enable all pupils with SEN to integrate into the county's planned tertiary provision;

- to review and develop the county's provision for pupils with a physical handicap – particularly in the primary phase. This development to be related to the return of pupils from out-county placements;
- to develop further the county's SLD residential facilities to provide appropriate opportunities for pupils to acquire independent living skills;
- to develop the education authority's input into the All Wales strategy for the mentally handicapped;
- to increase the education social work service to provide appropriate support for all high school feeder primaries and special schools (under the new child protection procedures and implications of the Elton Report and the new Children Act).

As a consequence of these aims leading on to objectives and targets, a costing exercise was undertaken whereby the annual cost of each targeted item was stated in the development plan so that a list of priority options could be constructed by the members for the forthcoming financial year.

THE CHANGING AIMS AND OBJECTIVES FOR SPECIAL NEEDS

The type and amount of provision is to some extent contingent on any local authority's overall business plan and what budget allocation is given to special needs services and schools over a period of time. It has long been the contention of advocacy groups that provision under statementing is pegged to resources. This is a critical problem for special needs provision, or indeed any provision given to schools by authorities. It is true that as local education authority development plans are made, annual position statements and budgets raised, with a cycle of options given, so provision can alter and, as policy develops, different priorities and emphases can be undertaken. Over a ten-year period as a senior manager and budget holder in special needs, I was involved in this process of policy implementing options. Examples of these policy decisions were changing pupil/teacher ratios, developing extra support for TVEI, or giving positive discrimination to small rural primary schools. Policy emphases at other key times were made for pre-school and nursery provision. Continuous programme options for staff development of special needs co-ordinators by secondment or INSET development was made throughout this period.

A capital building programme designed to adapt magnet schools in key areas to integrate physically handicapped pupils was a further implemented option target area. The return of deaf and blind children

to home-based schools from outside the authority, with the consequent virement of finance from one budget to another, was also
undertaken. The closure of some special schools with further virement
of staff and capitation to mainstream schools was implemented during
this period. All of these items were part of the longer-term developmental cycle and subject to strategic management over a period of
years. Most of these aims and objectives were incorporated into a
medium-term action programme and set out as part of a four-year
1989–92 'business plan'.

This developmental cycle of audit, objectives, targeting and review
was subject to the inevitable pressure caused by the demands of
changing legislation and the constant flow of circulars from the
Department of Education and Science, in particular Circulars 22/89
and 7/91 concerned with implementing varying aspects of the Education Reform Act 1988. As a consequence there has been a continuing
strategic review in all authorities of special needs aims and objectives.
A typical wide-ranging review was undertaken in 1991 in Clwyd to
address changing issues, such as service delivery, levels of statementing, the concept of a fully-resourced school under LMS and the
changing role of support services. After a report to the Education
Committee, this review produced a further set of strategic planning
aims and objectives and a fresh round of medium-term targets for the
county as a whole.

THE NEED FOR STRATEGIC DEVELOPMENT PLANNING

As local authorities carry out their responsibilities to formulate
policies on special needs, with inevitable rationalisation of provision
and in some cases with an increasing emphasis on integration, then
strategic management decisions and programmes for action will continue to be necessary in the 1990s. These plans and programmes
will inevitably mean displacement and retraining of staff, closure or
adaptations of schools, and reorganisation of support services. These
factors will need to be introduced into a strategic developmental programme and phased in over a period of time. It is certain that integration cannot be achieved by closing schools and placing children into
mainstream without considerable planning, preparation and training
before these things can be achieved.

OPPORTUNITY FOR GROWTH THROUGH STRATEGIC
DEVELOPMENT PLANNING

Growth can take place and objectives and aims can be realised. In the
1980s over a period of ten years the overall budget for special needs

rose from £3.5 million to £7.5 million in Clwyd, allowing for inflation. This was achieved by strategic planning in using the annual budget cycles, so that two political administrations over this period achieved many of the objectives for special needs contained in their business plans. An example of this, as with most authorities, was the growth in the school psychological service from eight to 19 staff, together with a senior management structure. Comparable developments also took place in support service provision. Of course, such developments need to be compared with the achievements of the previous decade when, as with many other local authorities, very significant special needs and special education developments took place. This was particularly so in capital expenditure programmes at schools for severe learning difficulty children, when in 1974 the newly formed LEAs took over responsibility from area health authorities for such children. There was also growth in new facilities for the deaf and children with behaviour disorders in separate schools or as units in mainstream primary and secondary schools.

Such strategic developments as these have created major dilemmas for many authorities who are reluctant to close down such recent provision, to meet policy changes in pursuit of, for example, integration programmes.

THE NEED FOR NATIONAL STRATEGIC PLANNING ARISING FROM THE ERA

Strategic planning at the centre will inevitably influence development planning at the circumference. The consequences of the developments in the 1970s and 1980s was that there were clear differences in provision between authorities, and in many cases within authorities. As a result there was no common currency of provision, and the definition of special needs in the Education Act 1981 of 'a child having special needs if special provision needs to be made' is a relative term interpreted in different ways and at different levels in different areas. Thus the Audit Commission Report (1992) shows that there can be a 3 per cent difference and probably even more between authorities in their statementing thresholds for special needs provision.

The great advantage of the Education Reform Act, with a common curriculum for all and with the emphasis on access, is that it brings about the need for explicit educational criteria for identifying pupils with special needs and with local management and places a responsibility on schools to be involved in such identification and to facilitate appropriate provision.

The problem is that unless clear moderation procedures are identified with clear and agreed criteria for identification, there will be an unseemly rush for statementing with the emphasis on 'greed rather than need'. It is clear that the pressure is upon local education authorities at this time to hold the ground on criteria and find a common currency and agreed formula for identification in statementing and provision.

As mentioned earlier, a recent House of Commons Select Committee (January 1993), looking at such moderation procedures, clearly raised fundamental questions about the criteria for statementing. Amongst further questions asked in their consultation were, at what level of need should children be statemented? What are the main reasons for the wide variation in the proportion of children with statements in different LEAs, and what steps are necessary to separate statements of need and statements of provision to reflect the purchaser provider model? Once such questions are answered the problems of evaluation and monitoring will also clearly be on the agenda, with ways needed for allowing parents to exercise choice for sometimes very expensive provision. When such provision is available, some equity in the use of resources in the face of demands for such expensive provision for different groups also needs to be established on national basis.

THE DEVELOPMENT CYCLE AND AUDITING SPECIAL NEEDS

Various approaches to such identification and categorisation of special needs have been undertaken by LEAs. For some, such categorisation reduces the concept of special needs to 'labelling children' and adopting practices used before the Warnock Report.

Nevertheless, the concepts of mild, moderate and severe learning difficulties are clearly with us as seen in Circular 11/90, which has attempted to band children into such levels of need for staffing purposes. As a consequence, there is a strong move in some authorities for the setting up of registers of need and clear regulation of categories of needs across various bands.

Such bands of need have been adopted in Kent, where an audit of each school's needs are moderated by attendance of school representatives/headteachers at panel meetings.

Northampton has adopted similar bandings, with sub-bands within these bands for the differing categories of communication difficulties, physical and sensory difficulties and emotional and behavioural difficulties. A statementing threshold from band two to band three has been established. For moderation purposes, all schools are required to provide a list of pupils which is moderated by educational psychologists working with support teachers across the county. Bands of need in stages 1 to 2 would be for children with marginal to mild degrees of special needs, with specialised support either on an individual or small group basis two or three times a week in band two. The school's special needs co-ordinator plays a key role at these stages. Bands three to six cover the range of sensory–physical and behavioural problems ranging from significant to severe difficulties. All of these bands require a statement to be made and all require formula funding from band four onwards with an average of one teacher and one qualified assistant to between eight to ten pupils on an age weighted basis. From this arrangement a special needs, age weighted pupil unit, SNAWPU, is generated. The setting for such provision can be flexible, allowing for the same staffing ratios to be in either reduced size, mainstream classes, or units, or special school settings. However, the bands are more sophisticated than this and can include provision for specialist consultation, a differentiated curriculum (academic, personal and social) and the use of equipment. Monitoring is undertaken for all children on bands three to six through the annual review procedures.

These descriptors then set out the education arrangements required for pupils in each band. Each can then be translated into group sizes, ratios of pupils to teachers and support assistants, materials, and curriculum arrangements. These can then be costed and related to the current LMS unit of resource. As a consequence, the total weighting for each pupil/place for a particular band/pupil type would be set to deliver a sufficient resource to provide what the descriptors require. Finally, the age weightings are given (from the existing LMS formula) so that a special needs and pupil type weighting is set, and so that age weighing × special needs weighting × pupil type weighting = total weighting required.

Another approach to auditing, as mentioned in a previous chapter, is the development of special needs registers. In Clwyd this uses the Warnock stages 1–5 of special needs using stage 5 level of need as a statementing threshold. These registers are maintained and moderated by special needs support teams comprising educational psychologists, senior special needs support teachers, special school outreach, individual school co-ordinators of special needs and, where necessary, area health and social service personnel. Such registers of special needs (see Table 6.1) can be used not only for auditing and allocating resources to schools as part of the formula for funding, but also to maintain the annual review of statements in the mainstream and to facilities reviews at 14 years to cover arrangements under the Disabled Persons Act 1986.

As these registers have been developed to accommodate the Education Reform Act 1988, they have begun to reflect National Curriculum attainment records, coupled with selected attainment tests in reading and number, and contain the varying screening devices used by the authority over the years. The requirements of Circular 22/89

Table 6.1 *Clwyd special needs team meetings*

School
Register/agenda/action sheet (4)   *Date:* 1 November 1990

Name of child	DOB	CA	Year	Stage	Special needs report (Attainment)						Action
					Sp + L	R	W	Sp	HW		
Liam	18.8.81		5	2	Sp + L	L2		L2		Reading: Hummingbirds Series (Group 2) Young Group Reading Test 29.10.90 RA 81; RQ 89; CA – 9.2 Blackwell Spelling Test SA 6.8 Working on Blackwell Spelling Workshop (Red Phase) 'Alpha to Omega' dictation. Careless – misses out words. Coping adequately but slowly and lacking in motivation.	1. Support to continue, concentrating on key spelling, complete first hundred. 2. Real books for stimulating motivation 3. 'Spelling Made Easy' introductory level. 4. Blackwell Spelling Workshop – extend to orange phase.
Carl	30.4.81		5	1	Sp + L	L2	TW L2	TW L2	TW L2	Progress in class is steady, but on the slow side. He needs motivating constantly.	1. Continue to monitor in class providing appropriate work in English and mathematics. 2. Regular reviews via staff meetings.

				Sp + L	R	W	Sp	HW	Support to continue
Shaun	1.6.82	4	2	L2a d	L2	WT L2	L2 b & c		1. Reading skills.

Key words 1st 100; R 92/100; S 41/60

Oxford Junior Work Book 3 – good progress

Reading: Trog series' – Finding these books interesting. Working on initial blends. Failing on ch, sh, sn, st. Final blends st, mp satisfactory.

Making own book to complement class topic.

Working hard in class. Attendance improved.

Support to continue
1. Reading skills.
2. Phonic development and spelling skills through 'Spelling Made Easy' introductory level; sounds in sentences; 'Sounds, Pictures and Words' Book 3.
Spelling – complete first 100 words. Reading being second 100 words.

on assessment under the National Curriculum have also been included. Such registers continue to be modified as further attainment tests come on stream under the National Curriculum arrangements at ages 7, 11 and 14. Children are supported by the special needs services at the different levels or by the schools themselves as more delegated funding has been allocated to buy in support service time and personnel.

Cumbria County Council (1992) have issued a special needs manual of practice with an even more closely defined audit. The criteria for statementing are based on degrees of learning difficulties and written with curriculum and developmental factors in mind. Statementing thresholds are again seen to be moderate, severe or profound, which attracts staffing support based on the model found in the DES Circular 11/90, *Staffing for Pupils with Special Educational Needs*. This has been translated at 1992 prices into a funding formula of £2,000 for moderate, £4,000 for severe and £6,000 for profound learning difficulties. Accumulative needs, which are called 'complex', provide funding of £8,000, and 'multiple', funding of £10,000 per child. So for example, to meet the criteria for statements in the moderate banding for a reading delay, the child has to be in year two or above and have a reading accuracy or comprehension score at or below the second centile, with a reading age of 9 years 6 months being the lowest point. Similar models are developed for spelling, handwriting and number attainments, where the criterion for the latter, as a statementing threshold, is again at or below the second centile. Cumbria has developed a greater number of statementing criteria for the various levels across a range of handicapping conditions including speech and language disorders, sensory disorders (with some very detailed criteria) and emotional and social difficulties. All of these criteria require a high degree of concentrated assessment at the school and support service level, and present some considerable moderation problems.

It is apparent therefore from these example that nationally agreed measures for identification in special needs and a framework in which the auditing procedures of such identification can be fitted are needed. The Department for Education have commissioned a national study of good practice in 1993. If such measures in such a framework can be agreed, then identification and quantification of the size of the population of special needs children can be undertaken. Once such a framework exists the regulation, identification and assessment of children, using agreed procedures, can be organised. The indices used should be valid and reliable so that objective decisions and consistent judgements can be made about pupils with similar difficulties in different schools.

As indicated under policy formulation, such procedure would also cover issues such as cross-authority moderation, statementing and annual review procedures and further issues such as parental requests for assessments and pre-school identification and assessment. It is becoming clearer that national policies and procedures are needed in this area.

As we have seen, the distinctive feature of a development plan is that it brings together in an overall plan national and LEA policies, the authority's aims and values, and its existing achievements and needs for development. Priorities for development can be planned in detail for some years and can be supported by action plans with aims and objectives for staff. The priorities for later years can be sketched in outline to provide the longer-term programme.

Further, the development plan captures the long-term vision of an authority within which manageable short-term goals are set. The priorities contained in the plan represent the authority's translation of policy into its agenda for action. This will enable the local authority to put its own policy plans into practice and allocate resources equitably. It is clear therefore that an audit of the extent of special needs and the criteria for identifying special needs is necessary.

AUDITING FOR SPECIAL NEEDS AT THE SCHOOL LEVEL

With these factors in mind, we can turn to the question of audit at the school or service level. Clearly an audit for special needs is part of the wider audit undertaken by the school. As part of the government's drive to raise the quality of education, every school is required to submit a development plan to its LEA. By co-ordinating those aspects of planning which might appear to be separate the school acquires a shared sense of direction. In this respect therefore a whole school approach to development is created with regard to such special needs issues as integration and differentiating the curriculum. Although ownership of development plans by all the staff and the governors is an important factor, the process of formulating the plan should involve staff in co-ordinated decision making. Holly and Southworth (1989) describe the development plan 'as an external contract between the school and the LEA and a internal contract between the staff and the headteacher' (see Figure 6.2 for the various characteristics of such a plan).

An audit will reveal where there are priorities needed for development, and these may have to be planned in detail for one year and supported by action plans, objective targets and performance indicators for the staff concerned. Priorities for later years can be outlined for longer-term programmes.

A school audit of special needs will need to take account of what is regarded as generally available within an authority in terms of

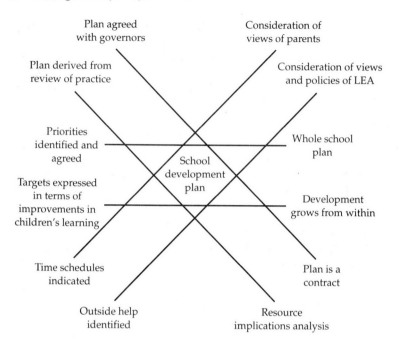

Figure 6.2 *Summary of characteristics of school development plans*

Source: Holly and Southworth (1989), p. 44

provision and resources so that central funding will be equitable. This will cover such areas as the school environment and adaptability, the teaching and learning approaches used, and a differentiated plan for the curriculum. Key staff appointments, such as a special needs co-ordinator or governor responsible for special needs schools, with plans for staff development to facilitate a whole school approach to special needs are also necessary. Cross-referencing of the school special needs policy to other policy documents is important. Informal audits within departments in a school can be undertaken by SWOT analyses, particularly where small numbers of staff are involved. So a consideration of the strengths, weaknesses, opportunities and threats can be undertaken in any area.

As mentioned at the beginning of this chapter, an alternative method of audit or review is GRIDS (guide-lines for the review of initial development in schools), which canvasses the views of staff by means of a questionnaire. Such questionnaires can also incorporate elements of the SWOT analysis. Major priorities requiring audit which are needed annually are curriculum provision and resources. This requires an annual curriculum return to be submitted to the LEA and the Secretary of State. Special needs curriculum issues will be among the priorities for development in this area.

The special needs working party in a secondary school and the special needs co-ordinator in a primary school should be responsible for co-ordinating special needs issues in a school audit on curriculum and resources. Roles, responsibilities and time-scales of the audit will need to be included in any development planning.

So how do I go about completing the audit in my school? The Education Department of Kent County Council (1992) set out the following guide-lines for special needs audits using their audit pro-formas. It was essential that all staff were well briefed on the process. it was also particularly important that the audit form was explained to them, possibly as a whole staff group, and that the relationship between evidence for the moderation of special needs and subsequent financing was fully understood.

The guide-lines suggested that some schools may find it more convenient to carry out their audit through departmental meetings. Others may wish to save discussion time by asking each class teacher to fill in the form in pencil first. This could then be discussed at a department meeting, or a meeting of the teacher with the person responsible for the audit. A brief in-service session, with the staff group discussing two or three pupils together, may help clear the way for a more speedy audit.

Another plan for schools would be to discuss what is required with all staff, then for departments or all the staff to work on two or three examples to gain confidence. Such audits can be carried out by the class teacher and cross-checked in the department or with the person responsible for the audit. The headteacher can review a sample of cases to ensure consistency, sampling across class and year groups and acting as an internal moderator. The class teachers of the special needs pupils to be moderated can then collate the evidence. If good records of assessments, target setting and review are kept this will present no problem.

Finally, each school could submit to the authority a summary sheet giving pupil name or number and level audited, the sample for moderation with children's supporting work and a total requirement for each level of need. As a consequence of these audits, a prioritised development plan for individual schools can be constructed for their special needs population. The special needs registers used in Clwyd after auditing each school's needs by numbers of children in each case identified what needed to be provided and how it was to be provided, with a monitoring of the effectiveness of the outcomes for each child.

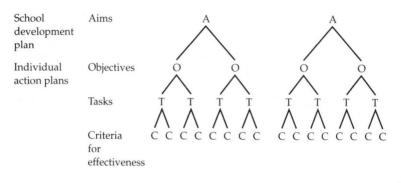

School
development
plan

Individual
action plans

Aims

Objectives

Tasks

Criteria
for
effectiveness

Figure 6.3 *Action plan cycle*

FROM AUDIT TO OBJECTIVES

As a consequence of such an audit, school development plans would
then contain a number of action plans which are translated into objectives, tasks and criteria for effectiveness (see Figure 6.3). The progression from aims to objectives will almost certainly be affected by
external and internal changes in a school, such as staff changes and
national and local policies.

The quality of the management of these changes in any planning
cycle is a key factor in successful development. Clearly, a model needs
to be used that emphasises and encourages co-operation and effective
co-ordination at all levels.

Ownership of the development plan by all the staff and the governors of a school is seen as a critical feature in such planning. So the
process of formulating the plan, as with the mission strategy, should
involve staff in co-ordinated decision making at different levels for
which a democratic decentralised style of school management is
desirable. As Stiles (1992) indicates, establishing a broadly-based
approach in which the views of the stakeholders are sought and taken
into account extends the ownership of the plan and makes it more
likely that its targets will be achieved. This process consists of both
short-term targets and longer-term thinking and planning and contains a number of key characteristics (see Figure 7.1 on page 94).

THE WHOLE SCHOOL APPROACH AS AN OBJECTIVE FOR
SPECIAL NEEDS

An example of a special needs area within a development plan is the
aim of developing a whole school approach as a way of meeting

special educational needs in the ordinary school. The purpose of this is to utilise the expertise of the staff and resources already existing in the school. To achieve a consistent approach to all children irrespective of need, agreed procedures and objectives need to be targeted. This is necessary to ensure staff consistency towards assessment and recording of children's work, towards the support needed for children with learning difficulties, and in providing a differentiated approach across all curriculum areas.

Amongst the key aims needed to develop a whole school approach at the secondary level would be the following:

- appointing at a senior level a special needs co-ordinator;
- setting up a special needs subgroup representing the governing body;
- there would be a need to establish an inter-departmental special needs group. Such a group would set targets for inter-group liaison meetings and the development of differentiated learning materials across and within the subject areas;
- there may be a need to review and recast the role of the special needs department to act as a support service to both pupils and staff across the school. To provide a range of opportunities which will stretch from the development of appropriate curriculum materials to the monitoring of individual pupils.

Table 6.2 shows how such aims can be turned into objectives and targets.

Once development plans have been laid out in terms of aims and objectives, related activities need to be put into effective action to complete the planning cycle. This requires the process of altering existing practice in order to achieve more effectively those desired curriculum outcomes for individual special needs pupils. Carrying out such tasks requires constant motivation, support and a clear allocation of resources in order to encourage involvement and effort on the part of those involved. A key managerial task where the special needs co-ordinator comes into focus is to maintain the participation level of all concerned throughout this phase.

Certain criteria are necessary to measure progress and report success, to indicate whether goals have been reached or at least that the school is moving in the right direction. The purpose of evaluation is for accountability and feedback aimed at improvement. Success criteria or measures, known as 'indicators', are therefore needed to assess performance.

Table 6.2 *Development plan for a whole school approach to special needs*

Aims	Objectives to be attained by date	Targets to be set for date
Support of the senior management and governors of the school	Discussion at senior management team/governors' meetings	Included in the whole school development plan
Appointment of special needs co-ordinators at a key level	Special needs co-ordinator develops termly liaison meetings with heads of subject departments	Monitoring the outcomes of the development plan for a WSA within the planning cycle
Presenting the school plan and strategy for whole school approach	Devising a clear strategy for monitoring the need for change WSA evident to all staff	Disseminating discussion paper on the changes needed
Devising a broad, balanced, differentiated curriculum for all	Differentiation planning in subject areas and forming a curricular planning team	Developing INSET activities for subject speculation in differentiation planning. Readability schemes in all subject areas with target dates

7

Quality of performance

The good is often the enemy of the best.

THE PRESSURE FOR QUALITY

The call for quality in education has been mentioned several times already in this book. In fact, the buzz-word in all sections of the public and private sectors is 'quality'.

We have considered policy and development planning and examined the way local management is being applied to the area of special education needs, but results are perhaps the first thing we look for when trying to evaluate an organisational activity, judging results as 'good', 'bad' or 'indifferent'. At the present time the education world abounds with talk of quality control, examination results, league tables, charters for parents, and appraisal for teachers. Circular 7/91 raises the issue of monitoring performance in special needs repeatedly and *Getting the Act Together* (Audit Commission, 1992b) discussed monitoring, first, the outcomes of policy statements both at the authority and school level, second, the effective use of delegated resources to mainstream schools, and third, the performance of teachers with pupils of lower ability. The earlier Audit Commission document, *Getting in on the Act* (1992a), indicated that neither special schools nor ordinary schools are called to give serious account of their performance with pupils with special needs, with the result that schools go virtually unchallenged on their work in this area. One could argue that improvement, quality and raising standards have always been the business of education, and that since the Callaghan debate in the 1970s followed by *Better Schools* in 1986 and the Education Reform Act 1988, improving quality has been the main thrust of educational reform. It is clear that authorities, services and schools are in the process of a cultural change, with an emphasis on 'getting close to the customer' into total quality management, by being clearer about the form and direction of special needs provision.

THE STAKEHOLDERS IN QUALITY OF PERFORMANCE

The total quality management philosophy provides a very strong challenge to some traditional attitudes on the part of service deliverers. It makes customer (service-user) judgements the ultimate criterion of performance, and what is more, it implies that the organisation has a responsibility to seek these out in advance in order to prevent mistakes before they occur rather than try to cure them afterwards. The policy in Clwyd of providing detailed but simple guide-lines of special needs provision and procedures brought the authority into close proximity with service users at the early stages of intervention and assessment and resulted in only two (unsuccessful) appeals in eight years of statementing.

We therefore need to ask, what do we want to do and need to do to achieve our objectives, what are our performance requirements, and is our service effective in dealing with special needs children and their parents?

Clearly, such questions tap the value system of authorities and schools, and such values, as discussed earlier, will determine an approach to quality and performance. So discussions on performance need to be set in the context of an organisation's values, mission, aims and objectives.

There are clearly difficulties in setting performance indicators for schools when one considers that there are differing stakeholders in the process. Different constituencies and different schools may require different measures of performance. Management in the public sector is set in a world in which many stakeholders seek to achieve their aims. There is a need to seek a balance in a continuing process. The conflicting interests are never fully satisfied but it is this search for balance that management has to develop, particularly in education. Central government provides measures for parents in its citizen's charters and by publishing results of schools' performance, thereby clearly indicating that these are key factors in measuring school effectiveness. Housden (1992) makes the point that with our peculiar national construction of quality in education, there is chronic under-achievement across the system, so that the dominant view powerfully reasserted of late by the government is that large-scale failure becomes a positive performance indicator. Teachers and educationists will criticise such league tables as reinforcing unfairness in only measuring outcomes and not considering the value-added factors provided by the schools.

THE EFFECTIVE SCHOOL

Increasing parental choice, raising of competitiveness and consumerism is being fostered for parents by the charters. This, together with the mechanics of local management of schools, means that some performance indicators for effective schooling, which schools and staff might wish to use for their own educational management purposes, have been displaced by the tabloid priorities. As a consequence, although schools have repudiated quantitative indicators they have not devised more robust systems of accountability and this has left a vacuum that has been filled with raw results.

In a government publication *Secondary Schools: Analysis of the Best Two Hundred Schools* (DES, 1988a), 12 criteria were set out for the effective school:

- good leadership – by heads, deputies, departmental and pastoral staff;
- clear aims and associated objectives translated into classroom practice, implemented and monitored;
- emphasis on high academic standards, encouraging all pupils to achieve to their full potential;
- a relevant, but orderly and firm, classroom atmosphere;
- good relationships with pupils who were encouraged to express views, understood the purposes of lessons and were strongly motivated;
- a coherent curriculum, well planned and implemented and serving the needs of pupils;
- concern for pupils' development as individuals in society, with a commitment by staff to their personal and social development and effective guidance;
- well-qualified staff, with experience and expertise, skilfully deployed and in receipt of appropriate development and training;
- suitable and respected working accommodation with appropriate specialist rooms and an aesthetically stimulating environment;
- effectively deployed and managed material resources;
- good relationships with community, parents and governors;
- the capacity to manage change, solve problems and develop organically.

MONITORING SCHOOL EFFECTIVENESS

Addressing these issues will help to change perceptions and enable schools and authorities to be pro-active, as Clwyd has been, in the setting of quality controls for all their schools and services based on

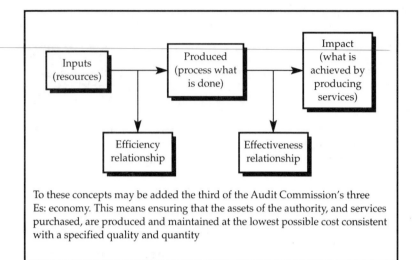

To these concepts may be added the third of the Audit Commission's three
Es: economy. This means ensuring that the assets of the authority, and services
purchased, are produced and maintained at the lowest possible cost consistent
with a specified quality and quantity

Figure 7.1 *Policy process on school effectiveness: stage 1*
Source: Clwyd LEA

Table 7.1 *Policy process on school effectiveness: stage 2*

Input Data	Process PIs	Output PIs
Student 'quality' resources: • buildings • finance • personnel • LEA support	School level Classroom level	Student performance

Source: Clwyd LEA

qualitative as well as quantitative factors and allowing for the
input – process – outcome model of quality control to be used. Figure
7.1 outlines Clwyd's policy on school effectiveness and the monitoring
dimension, whilst Table 7.1 takes it into the next stage. Table 7.2 considers the general distribution of the input–process–outcome model in
performance monitoring.

The purpose of monitoring is to increase the quality of education.
This seems to mean two things: first, that student outcomes (e.g.
academic, personal and social), and second, the internal conditions
of schools (e.g. the teaching/learning process, the capacity for change)
are improved. The best available knowledge from the school improvement literature suggests that to achieve these ends will require that

Table 7.2 *Input–process–outcome model in performance monitoring*

Inputs

Area of monitoring	Examples of data
Students	1. Achievements in standardised tests on entry. 2. Socio-economic background. 3. Ethnic background. 4. Pupil attitude on entry.
Buildings	1. Area per pupil. 2. Specialist provision per pupil. 3. Leisure provision per pupil. 4. Age of buildings.
Finance	1. Total per pupil from LEA. 2. Total per pupil from other sources.
Staff	1. PTR. 2. Qualifications. 3. Age profile. 4. Experience. 5. Relationship of employment to appropriate qualification.
Parental support	1. Number of hours per pupil given to support school.
LEA support	1. Degree of adviser support.

Processes

Area of monitoring	Examples of possible performance indicators
Academic emphasis	1. Rate of homework set, done and marked. 2. Rate of awards for excellence. 3. Curriculum time devoted to 'basics'. 4. Provision for gifted pupils.
Classroom management	1. Rate of time spent interacting with class. 2. Rate of pupil progress feedback. 3. Extent to which praise is given.
Pupil conditions	1. Expenditure per head on buildings upkeep. 2. Outstanding repairs each month. 3. Rate and nature of pupils' accidents.
School management	1. Time spent in meetings discussing curriculum. 2. Time spent by management per member of staff in observation.
Clear goals and monitoring	1. Rate of staff awareness of goals. 2. Extent of pupil monitoring systems.
Staff development	1. Rate of attendance at INSET. 2. Perception of quality of INSET.
LEA support	1. Perception of quality of support.
Parental involvement	1. Rate of attendance at meetings.

Table 7.2 *cont*

Area of monitoring	Examples of possible performance indicators
Parental involvement cont	2. Opportunities per year for involvement. 3. Rate of attendance at all activities.
Pupil groupings	1. Rate of setting/mixed ability. 2. Average group sizes by age/subject.
Curriculum	1. Number of subjects provided. 2. Percentage of time per subject. 3. Rate of teacher hours on SEN.
Staff	1. Contact ratios. 2. Percentage of staff teaching specialism. 3. Attendance rates. 4. Turnover rates.
Accommodation	1. Rate of utilisation. 2. Furniture expenditure per pupil. 3. Energy expenditure per pupil. 4. Cleaning cost per pupil.
Finance	1. Capitation expenditure per pupil. 2. Capitation expenditure per subject. 3. Administration expenditure per pupil. 4. Teacher expenditure per pupil. 5. Non-teaching staff cost per pupil.
Pastoral	1. Percentage staff time spent on pastoral work. 2. Rate of pupil perception of quality of work.

Outputs

Area of monitoring	Examples of possible indicators
Intellectual/skill development	1. Performance measured at development 7+, 14+, 16+, 18+.
Social development	1. Rate of pupil attendance. 2. Rate of lateness. 3. Rate of exclusions and suspensions. 4. Rate of satisfaction expressed by outsiders.
Emotional development	1. Rate of participation in community activity. 2. Rate of participation in caring activities.
Physical development	1. Rate of participation in extracurricular sport. 2. Rate of success in competitions.
Propensity towards lifelong learning	1. Rate of FE participation.
Relationship with industry	1. Rate of entry to employment/YTS. 2. Rate of employment status three years after leaving.

performance indicators are linked to a school's own monitoring via school development planning, as was indicated in Chapter 6.

The lessons of school effectiveness research suggest that the factors which characterise effective or high-attaining schools, having allowed for pupil intake variation, are:

Academic emphasis
- high academic expectations by teachers;
- a belief that all students can learn;
- a belief that teachers can teach;
- regular setting and marking of homework;
- visible rewards for academic excellence;
- a particular emphasis on reading, writing and maths.

Classroom management
- lesson time spent on task;
- a high proportion of teacher time spent interacting with the class, not individuals;
- lessons beginning and ending on time;
- clear feedback to pupils on progress and expectation;
- ample praise for good performance;
- minimal disciplinary intervention;
- focus on only one curriculum area in a lesson;
- closely structured lessons.

Pupil conditions
- a safe and orderly climate;
- building in good order of repair and decoration;
- pupil participation in the running and organisation of the school.

School management
- a focus by the headteacher on classroom instruction and learning;
- direct observation by the headteacher of classroom activity;
- collaborative staff planning.

Clear goals and monitoring
- all staff know the goals;
- priorities are set for staff;
- pupil progress is continually monitored against goals.

The economy, efficiency, effectiveness and, not least as far as special needs is concerned, equity dimension, all need to be in focus in any considerations of measuring quality at central government, LEA, school, teacher, or service levels. Table 7.3 highlights this factor in a value chain.

Table 7.3 *Value chain in performance monitoring*

	Central government	LEA	School	Teacher/ practitioner
Economy	Resources	LMS	Allocation of resources	Use of resources
Efficiency	Allocation in relation to 'needs' as opposed to 'politics'	Support services	Resource–output issues, 'environment' factors (contracts)	Resource to needs
Effectiveness	Legislation policy e.g. National Curriculum	Support to education process advisers, etc.	Use of staff learning programmes	Learning outcomes
Equity	Policy legislation, strong social concern	Policies and actual values	Policies and positive discrimination values	Practise what is preached

THE EFFECTS OF LOCAL MANAGEMENT OF SCHOOLS ON PERFORMANCE MONITORING

There is a duty in the local management of schools for school governors to issue annual reports and arrange annual meetings for parents to account for the workings of the school. Such reports include financial statements on the school budget and a statement of the work of the school in terms of assessments and examination results. With the requirement of a special needs governor for all schools, it should be expected that a special needs dimension is included in such annual reviews of the school's progress. The duty of governors in reporting and the rights of parents to receive information is an illustration of the new rights and responsibilities of key stakeholders under the LMS partnership. Of course, what governors report will in part be influenced by the LEA, the headteacher and the staff of the school, and in the effective school all the parties should be consulted concerning recommendations for suitable performance indicators. So the quality of performance indicators under local management will depend upon the involvement of the key partners and their links with the values, aims and purposes of the school. The way performance is reported and the methods of communication may well be a factor in the marketing of the school, a topic discussed in Chapter 8.

Performance review is clearly part of the good management and quality control issue in education. However, there are other factors which provide an impetus for such review as the recent report *Getting the Act Together* (Audit Commission, 1992b) demonstrates.

THE EFFECT OF DELEGATION OF SERVICES ON QUALITY

There is a need for accountability for provision of services in special needs. Are resources allocated under LMS being used efficiently and are they effectively being directed towards the area intended? Are the resources allocated being used so that policy aims, for example in integration, are being realised? Performance review can enhance such accountability by highlighting aspects of service provision where further enquiry and explanation is needed. It can also explicitly target the responsibilities and achievements of individual members of staff in a school, service or local authority as the policy review from the recent Audit Commission (1992c) analysis in Lincolnshire indicated.

Lincolnshire LEA's special needs policy set out objectives for the special needs service. One of them was to place an increasing proportion of pupils with moderate learning difficulties in ordinary schools until the majority were educated there. Services which increase the capability of ordinary schools in educating pupils with special needs were a priority for resources. Progress in the implementation of the policy was measured by the following indicators:

- pupil numbers in ordinary and special schools and special units;
- occupancy rates of special schools and units;
- pupil:teacher ratios;
- number of support staff in ordinary schools;
- number of pupils with statements;
- placement of pupils with statements;
- special school expenditure per pupil;
- expenditure per pupil in special units;
- expenditure on placements outside the LEA.

Each indicator was presented in a table showing trends over the last four years, enabling the elected members of the LEA to see the direction of change. Trends were also presented graphically. The Director of Education made an annual report to members on the progress made in implementing the policy. This report opened with a single paragraph which detailed the progress made in two or three important areas and ended with a detailed breakdown of the above statistics.

As more and more services and resources are being delegated under the local management schemes, with special schools being included by 1994, so increasing use of performance indicators will be needed to investigate why some schools are more effective than others, for example in developing a whole school approach to special needs, or achieving a higher level of exclusion of children with behavioural difficulties than another school in a similar catchment area.

Getting the Act Together (Audit Commission, 1992c, p. 47) indicated that many schools and LEAs are reluctant to use objective measures of school's performance in special needs because they believe that such indicators give only a partial impression of a school's work in this area and are therefore misleading.

THE FACTORS IN SETTING PERFORMANCE TARGETS FOR SPECIAL NEEDS

I have indicated elsewhere (Walters, 1992) that the Clwyd county policy and development plan, which included a school audit based on the special needs register, provided a means for monitoring children's schools, teachers and service performance. Through such registers of needs, levels of provision and support were accompanied by clear criteria for monitoring and review.

Certainly, the writing of statements at level 5 on this register, via a menu approach of clear objectives for children, with annual reviews reflecting the demands of the National Curriculum, goes some way to monitoring the performance of all the parties concerned and, by sending annual reviews prior to completion to parents for comment, included most of the stakeholders in the monitoring process. The increasing use of records of achievement across all sectors, including special schools (where Tyr Morfa Special School in Rhyl was a pioneer in this field) provided children with an opportunity to participate in their own quality control procedures. Thus a performance culture became widely accepted in the county with the key to this being clear policy statements, leading to clear objectives set out in a business plan with quality controls across all sectors including special needs.

Without a clear purpose and clear objectives derived from mission and policy, performance has no clear criteria to be judged against. A clear sense of an indicator of performance cannot be made unless there is identification of what objectives are in mind.

There needs to be laid down in the school management context a set of performance tasks in the following manner;

- performance tasks: what does he, she, it, do?
- performance statements: by what methods does he, she, it, do it?
- performance effectiveness: how well does he, she, it, do it?
- performance indicators: how do you measure what he, she, it, has done?

INDICATORS FOR PERFORMANCE FOR SPECIAL NEEDS IN THE MAINSTREAM

With these objectives in mind, the time has surely come to clarify the common ground between special and mainstream schools and to clarify the differences in performance tasks. Common tasks are clearly concerned with the National Curriculum, as it is common to all sectors. A major development is the school approach to differentiation of the curriculum, again using an input–process–outcome model. The increasing use of records of achievement, as mentioned earlier, could provide a common basis for tasks, statements, effectiveness and indicators once agreed national, local or within-school criteria are in place. There are a number of examples and criteria for performance measurement included at the end of this chapter, but an example following the above criteria for a mainstream high school adopting a whole school approach to special needs is suggested here.

Such a school structure is established through a policy in which the school has appointed a special needs co-ordinator at management level and a special educational needs committee, including a governor, overseeing a regular special needs inservice programme for key staff. The methods by which the co-ordinator and the committee carry out their tasks can be translated into performance statements; for example, by what methods does the co-ordinator oversee the statementing process, or how is the inservice delivered? Indicators of effectiveness can be set to ask questions as to how well this system is working, such as how well is the special educational needs committee proving to be an effective change agent for differentiating the curriculum? Has the inservice programme affected staff skills? From such questions, performance indicators can be set which are mathematical indicators, setting school-based targets. Such indicators might be: how many pupils still have difficulty because materials are still too complicated? How many other areas of the curriculum still need a differentiated approach? How much of the course materials in a subject area have been monitored for readability and the conceptual difficulties and access difficulties for children with sensory or physical disabilities? There are some useful indicators in this direction in the National Curriculum Council publication *A Curriculum for All* (NCC, 1989).

INDICATORS FOR PERFORMANCE IN SPECIAL SCHOOLS

From a special school point of view, with a developmental plan and policy committed to linking itself with a mainstream cluster of schools, a setting of tasks and statements concerned with integration and staff outreach would be agreed. This would focus on performance of such tasks at the school or teacher level in various areas. These could be: how often are staff involved in contracts with mainstream on outreach service contracts? What percentage of time across levels of need are pupils spending in functional integration opportunities from the special school? What is the frequency of parental involvement in integration schemes on joint programmes for their children? (There are some valued-added factors here in terms of locality to schools and staff time available in liaison with parents.) How effective is the use of ancillary support in developing and monitoring individual educational programmes? The case of a handicapped infant school-child, over-protected by an ancillary, was exemplified at mealtimes when she regularly took the lid off his yoghurt cup in the dining-room. The other children at the table eventually asked 'Why don't you let him lick the lid like the rest of us, miss?' The eventual successful negotiation of the lid with the tongue, although slow, brought a chorus of cheers from the table: integration in action, performance negotiated.

A note of caution should be introduced here on statements and annual reviews which lead to individual educational programmes. It may be, as has happened in the USA and is beginning to surface in the UK, that parents may appeal and even turn to litigation when performance targets set for individual children by schools are not achieved. This has been particularly noticeable over dyslexic children. Is this a matter for teacher appraisal and will the ultimate outcome of performance indicators for individual schools result in the 'buck stopping' with individual teachers? It may be that the growth of performance-related pay and the development of appraisal procedures will result in a tiered system of teacher competence ratings. This may in turn result in the weeding out of unsuccessful teachers, or schools being forced to close because of their failure to meet national or local targets.

With regard to special schools, however, it is suggested there needs to be a different approach to school outcomes by providing for different areas of special needs. There will inevitably need to be differing criteria with strong attention to input and process indicators between schools for children with severe learning difficulties and schools catering for children with emotional and behavioural disorders. Special needs teaching is clearly concerned with inputs and the process of education, a qualitative rather than a quantitative approach. So in this connection it was sad to see some special schools being included at the bottom of league tables for exam results in the same division as grant-maintained schools. The effectiveness of such special schools is often seen in the confidence of the pupils and the levels to which they have developed a measure of autonomy and self-discipline. Such measures can be articulated through records of achievement, but whether these extend to the league table system waits to be seen. So often mainstream schools celebrate the few and mislead the many.

WHOLE SCHOOL APPROACHES TO INTEGRATION

Nevertheless, schools at the head of national league tables for examination results can also have vigorous whole school approaches to special needs and produce clear aims across a range of statements for action with clear indicators of performance. One such leading school, Parrswood High (Manchester City Council, 1992), has produced a range of indicators through its faculty of learning support action development plan, which includes curriculum development, community aims, staff development and budgeting objectives for special needs (see Table 7.4). Another such school, St George's, Tunbridge Wells, has produced a clear rationale for integration with performance areas for implementation (see Table 7.5).

This process of integration is very often not properly monitored for individual children when readability schemes or basic facilities are not clearly targeted. In my capacity as a Local Authority Inspector, I shadowed a special needs child for several days in a high school and found that many of the reading materials, books and worksheets had not been analysed for readability, so that the child, though capable of carrying out tasks in certain practical areas, was unable to do so because materials were some four years ahead of her reading age. Often the small things are important; another child was failing to achieve a reasonable level of part-time integration into a primary school because she did not have a peg in the cloakroom to hang her coat. As a consequence, she had to carry it round the school with her, which made her stand out from her peers, thus affecting her social integration.

STRATEGIC FACTORS IN PERFORMANCE PLANNING

Performance targets and indicators will need to be covered in LEAs' strategic planning and review procedures. As policy documents are being rewritten in the light of LMS(S) this is clearly a major issue for value systems as well as for policy and review. Integration will be seen as a hierarchy of provision, with movement of children between categories being targeted in a developmental planning exercise (see Table 7.6).

Special needs performance review and quality control can therefore be seen to be operative at all levels: at the authority level with policy reviews; at the school level with quality controls of delegated

Table 7.4 *Parrswood School: special needs performance indicators*

General aim

	Action	Performance indicators
To support the establishment of differentiated learning programmes enabling all students to achieve their potential.	1. Inservice sessions with subject faculties. 2. To be invited to and participate in subject faculties curriculum planning.	1. Differentiated resources packs available. 2. Evidence of differentiated teaching in the classroom.
To encourage flexible teaching styles across the curriculum.	Liaise with directors of faculty.	1. INSET sessions. 2. Materials modified and guidance given. 3. Input in subject faculty meetings. 4. Class input.
Heightened awareness of individual difficulties encountered by students.	Liaise with SM and timetabler.	1. Effective dissemination of information to staff. 2. Planning time reserved to discuss work with subject teachers being supported.

Student objectives

	Action	Performance indicators
To support students who have difficulty gaining full benefit from/access to the curriculum.	1. Proforma developed for subject staff. 2. Diagnostic testing. 3. Liaise and support classroom assistant.	1. Learning programmes in place for most/least able: a) individual, b) generalised. 2. Termly review of the role of the classroom assistant.
To screen all year 7 students via the Suffolk reading test.	1. Screen year 7. 2. Information disseminated to faculty directors.	1. Information used by faculty directors. 2. Diagnostic tests given to individual students. 3. Parent/tutor working with student.
Introduce Buddy reading scheme for year 7/8 students.	1. Introduce programme for sixth formers.	1. Scheme in place and monitored. 2. Termly review.
For statemented students to feel part of the annual review.	1. Student to be invited to review meeting. 2. Feedback received by teachers after meeting.	a) Presence of student at meeting. b) Information used to student's benefit.

Table 7.4 *cont*

To assess progress of students receiving additional support.	1. Student record card developed. 2. Discussion held with subject teacher.	1. Establish a school SEN register with priority/point system. 2. Student record card in use. 3. Subject teacher aware of amount of LS involvement.

Staffing and staff development objectives

To offer each member of faculty a professional development interview on an annual basis.	Calendar for interview.	1. Established priorities within faculty budget for current INSET needs. 2. Empathetic, happy team.
To appoint an additional member of the faculty with responsibility for the gifted.	To ensure this stays a 'high profile issue' with SMT and governors.	Colleague appointed.
To recognise and support the framework within which section 11 colleagues are required to work	1. Joint team meetings. 2. Participation in production of faculty policy and practice document. 3. Sharing of equipment.	1. Section 11 work programme in place supported, where appropriate, by LS faculty. 2. Time at faculty meetings allocated to section 11 issues. 3. Advice from section 11 staff on way forward.

Curriculum objectives

Students of all abilities to have the opportunity to experience success.	1. Advice given on production of differentiated materials. 2. Advise colleagues on the necessary modifications of SATs at KS3. 3. Arrange individual support for pupils in SATs.	1. Differentiated materials in place. 2. Range of work on display. 3. Successful participation in SATs for all pupils.

Table 7.4 *cont*

To illustrate by good practice a variety of flexible and differentiated teaching styles which cater for all abilities.	Produce INSET booklet on able student.	1. INSET booklet distributed to staff. 2. Evidence of good practice in the classroom. 3. Use of extension materials.
To support subject teachers in partnership.	LS to share workload in preparation/teaching/marking.	1. Shared materials in place. 2. Dual contribution at parents evening/ROAs.
To involve parental expertise in student learning programmes.	1. Letter to parents asking for help. 2. Develop a structured programme with training for parents. 3. Annual review of scheme by parents/students/teachers.	1. Programme development and in place. 2. Evaluation and development of programme.

Premises, supplies and service objectives

To create a resource centre which facilitates and supports the learning process for all students and supports a process of teaching and learning in the classroom.	1. Negotiate with SMT. 2. Budget bids.	1. Resource centre in place. 2. Resource centre used by students and staff.
To enhance computer provision for students.	1. Additional points in S12. 2. Budget bids for computers and software. 3. Bid for old BBC computers.	Additional computer in S12.
To ensure that all areas of the school are accessible to students irrespective of any physical disabilities.	1. Mapping of school. 2. SMT aware of need.	Ramps.

Table 7.5 *St George's School: analysis of integration stages*

Integration as a process	Integration in the community	Integration through group work	Integration on a part-time basis	Full integration in a mainstream school
The pupil is engaging in the equivalent opportunities and experiences that would be available in a mainstream school curriculum.	The pupil is experiencing liaisons with other schools through joint activities at a purely social level.	The pupil is involved in specific activities with mainstream pupils, such as joint activity days and leisure and sporting events.	The pupil attends a course specifically designed for their educational needs based in a mainstream school or college.	Full-time placement in a mainstream school with support from special school.
The pupil has a National Curriculum profile indicating attainment targets covered and at what level.	The pupil partakes in educational visits in the community through visits to local commercial and industrial organisations.	The pupil partakes in group activities in specific curriculum activities based in mainstream schools.	The pupil integrates on an individual basis for specific curriculum areas working alongside mainstream pupils.	Full placement without support.
	The pupil works alongside an adult other than a teacher from the community either in the confines of school or through work experience.		The pupil attends, with support, a mainstream school for: (i) half a day a week; (ii) one day a week; (iii) part of a week.	

This table describes the stages of integration used by St George's School, Tunbridge Wells, and could be seen to be measured elements of various stages in the integration process.

Table **7.6** *Performance indicators from policy statements*

Areas	Performance indicators
Special needs policy statement.	Reference to inclusive curriculum monitoring attainments to all pupils in relation to the curriculum offered gaining parental co-operation.
Statements of special needs.	Evidence that these are used as a starting point in learning programmes reviewed annually. Involve parents.
Whole school systems and procedures in operations in identification of learning requirements for all children.	Evidence of a school system/framework based on teachers' knowledge. Which is easy too.
System for monitoring children's attainments.	Is formative and uses Key stage assessment material. Is diagnostic: works at what children can do in relation to the curriculum and differentiates changes which are necessary.

resources; and at the service level, as the work of support service networks and teams are closely monitored and regulated.

PERFORMANCE INDICATORS FOR SUPPORT SERVICES

Support services throughout the educational system have been undertaking marketing audits on the range and nature of their support to schools and authorities and developing service agreements with their varying stakeholders. These efforts have resulted in a number of quality service contracts being drawn up, as mentioned earlier. An example can be seen with Cheshire's Learning Support Service, which has drawn up a comprehensive policy and development plan and introduced a programme of support more responsive to the needs of schools (Cheshire County Council, 1992). So for the staff concerned there has been agreement in developing at stage 1 a series of enabling indicators with a plan in place which addresses key service objectives. This has been followed by drawing up an agreement with all service staff that these key objectives need addressing, so that everyone is clear about their own targets and responsibilities. A number of outcome indicators have been introduced, such as improvement of time-scales between referral and response. There has been a positive feedback with an increased revenue from schools through the service agreement procedures. Schools are buying in more staff time for a wider range of needs. As part of the evaluation strategy monitoring

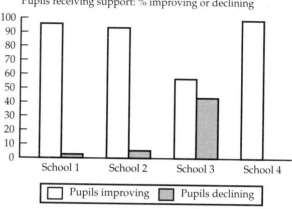

Pupils receiving support: % improving or declining

Figure 7.2 *Value for money from a support service*

Source: Audit Commission (1992b), p. 53

these targets, named individuals are nominated for co-ordinating strategies and evaluating success. Regular timetabled meetings are held by key managers to evaluate progress through contact with an ongoing sample of schools to monitor changes in their perceptions of the responsiveness of the service. Such an approach can overcome many of the problems revealed by the District Audit Service (Audit Commission, 1992b, p. 53), when they conducted a review of the value for money offered by the special needs support team in an LEA which it was auditing (see Figure 7.2).

The elected members of the LEA had resolved that the major priority for the service should be to help pupils make progress in literacy. It was reasonable to use the results of a test designed to measure pupils' progress in literacy (the Salford Sentence Test) as one indicator of the effectiveness of the support service. A more detailed investigation revealed that the problem in the school in question was one of poor co-ordination between the support teacher and the school. At the school's suggestion, the support teacher was carrying out work which did not focus on the development of literacy skills, and yet the pupils were being withdrawn from classes where they would otherwise have been focusing on literacy skills. This explains why they fell further behind in the area. Until this exercise was carried out, the LEA and school had been unaware of the impact of their approach.

Since the LEA did not have the resources to monitor the progress of every pupil receiving extra help from the service, the LEA and schools required management information of this kind to enable them to assess the effectiveness of the service overall, and to help decide where more detailed investigation was required.

In the same study, the District Audit Service (Audit Commission, 1992b) also questioned a sample of headteachers as to whether the support service had been helpful in enabling schools to develop their own skills in providing for pupils with special needs. Although a majority of them found the service helpful, they also found this aspect of the team's work to be indistinguishable from similar help provided by advisers and educational psychologists, a major problem for future support service managers. This is clearly an alternative form of performance monitoring available to LEAs and the Department for Education, as we discuss later in this chapter.

Finally, it would be possible to devise a whole range of performance targets, if not outcome indicators, for schools and services, and we have indicated earlier some evaluated by HMI. Indeed, a number of HMI surveys in very recent years on special needs have been undertaken. These include support services (DES, 1989b), integration into secondary and further education (DES, 1992), and National Curriculum developments in special schools (DES, 1991b). These all show a critical awareness of the strengths and weakness of special needs provision across a range of indicators with key guidelines for improvement.

THE ROLE OF GOVERNING BODIES IN PERFORMANCE MONITORING

Guide-lines for governors in checking for performance in special needs were reported by Doe and Kelly (1992) and contained the following check-lists to which governors should be able to answer 'yes':

- is there a whole school policy for special educational needs?
- is a senior member of staff responsible, with sufficient time?
- are there systems for detecting all children's special needs?
- are sufficient resources allocated to meet special needs?
- is there a nominated governor or teacher responsible for seeing that all teachers know about a child's difficulties?
- is there a regular check that all children participate fully in the curriculum and in extracurricular activities?
- is there a system for ensuring that all teaching takes account of special needs?
- is there a system for obtaining help from outside when the school cannot cope?
- are these policies adequately monitored?
- are parents treated as full partners?
- do governors receive anonymous reports on individuals so that they can judge if they are using their 'best endeavours'?

Governors must ensure that schools identify children's needs early enough and treat them seriously by:

- appointing a specific governor or group of governors to oversee special educational needs;
- requesting termly reports to the governing body on special needs;
- making all buildings physically accessible;
- allocating sufficient resources;
- appointing a senior teacher with responsibility for special needs;
- giving the pastoral side of the school a high priority;
- involving parents in their child's progress (or lack of it);
- ensuring that procedures for referring pupils who should have statement of special educational needs are widely known and that such pupils' needs are reviewed annually;
- ensuring outside specialist work with the staff to meet as many needs as possible within the school;
- ensuring admissions and disciplinary policies do not discriminate against pupils with special educational needs;
- maintaining close links with the local education authority special needs section and keeping members, officers and inspectors informed of success and areas of concern.

MONITORING THE QUALITY OF STATEMENTS FOR SPECIAL NEEDS

Amongst key performance issues in any exemplars given would be serious consideration of the matters raised by the House of Commons Select Committee on the role and value of statementing. There is already in place a six-month deadline on completion within the new Education Act, but clearly, whilst the Select Committee is seeking wider consultation on these matters, further parameters may well be set.

INDIVIDUAL EDUCATIONAL ATTAINMENT AS A PERFORMANCE INDICATOR

With so much attention being paid to audits of special needs at the school and authority level, as we have seen in authorities such as Kent, Cumbria and Northampton, attention may be given to similar detailed examination of individual children's progress. As a consequence, individual educational programmes in future may well become a key factor for monitoring the outcomes of some very significant financial inputs. In an increasing number of authorities large numbers of children with special needs are having their progress monitored, as in Clwyd, on special needs registers; those children on statements are monitored nationally on annual reviews. However, HMI (DES, 1989b), in reporting these procedures, have raised doubts on the quality of monitoring effectiveness. In many areas in the United States the measurement of learner outcomes is now very much in focus. For example, in Schools District 742 in Minnesota their strategy for excellence and equity (Minnesota Schools District, 1989) states that 'each student will receive instruction in the defined curriculum and the student's success will be evaluated through measures tightly aligned with the curriculum which will report measurable results of accomplishment'. So performance goals with learner outcomes are set against a wide range of criteria, both for areas of the curriculum covered and for support service inputs. In the curriculum areas, for example in language, arts and reading performance, goals are set at all grades from kindergarten to senior high exit levels with up to 35 performance goals set in any one grade. Assessments are then made with 80 per cent mastery in language and reading meeting the minimum criteria, 80 per cent to 87 per cent meeting and exceeding expectations, with test results below 80 per cent accuracy as not meeting expectations. Similarly, performance goals were set for support services involvement such as school psychological services. Performance goals were set for child, parental, staff and service responses, which were measured both by surveys and analysis of internal data. The graphic example shown in Figure 7.3 provides a three-year measure of the contact time psychologists spent on various types of activities.

An increasing number of children in the special needs system in England and Wales are on individual educational programmes which are made up of a series of stages and goals differentiated across the National Curriculum attainment target levels. The qualitative elements in these individual programmes are strongly emphasised by those in special needs education over and against quantitative outcomes.

PROBLEMS AND ISSUES IN SPECIAL NEEDS QUALITY ANALYSIS

There is a major dilemma facing quality management in the special education field for the future in setting realisable targets for children. The value-added factors of input differentiation procedures and process methodologies are critical before effective outcomes can be examined. There is an agreed curriculum within which all children operate, but the progress of the special needs child through that

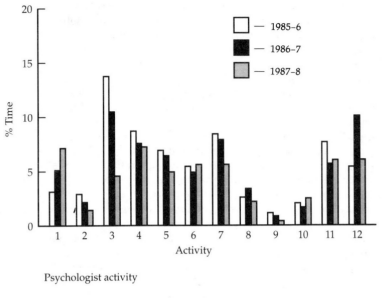

Figure 7.3 *Psychologist activity log*

Source: St Cloud (1989), p. 7

Psychologist activity

1. Student intervention
2. Observation
3. Assessment
4. Consultation
5. Staffings
6. Parent conferences
7. Reports
8. Background
9. Provide inservice
10. Receive inservice
11. Programme development psy services
12. Programme development other

curriculum and the outcomes achieved require different indicators to those currently in use through exam league tables.

To use performance indicators mechanically to point the finger at apparent failure is too simplistic. The mathematical accuracy of a few quantitative indicators can be spurious. What is clearly needed is a system of indicators which bear on all the significant criteria for judging effectiveness in special needs.

'The very value of Performance Indicators as a small number of key pieces of information is at the same time their limitation' (Eggar, 1988). Eggar went on to say that 'they can in no way offer a full judgement on a school's effectiveness. For this, one needs to examine a range of criteria through inspection procedures.' In this regard OFSTED (1992, p. 15), in their framework for the inspection of schools evaluation criteria, offer some alternative factors for the evaluation of special needs and for evidence of effective schooling:

- the number of pupils with special education needs (including those with statements) and the level of support for these pupils;
- a school policy for special educational needs;
- procedures used to achieve the objectives of this policy;
- access to, modification of and disapplication from the National Curriculum;
- staffing provision, including the use of external agencies;
- staff expertise and qualifications, INSET provision for staff at all levels;
- the use made of support teachers and service pupils for whom there is a statement of special educational needs;
- the extent of and appropriateness of integration within school;
- screening and assessment information and procedures;
- pupil groupings;
- the nature of specialist accommodation and resources, the extent of physical access for groups with special needs;
- the level of discussion with staff, pupils and parents on special needs;
- the involvement and discussion with medical, paramedical, nursing specialists and psychologists.

A report should include:

- an evaluation of the academic and social progress made and standards achieved by pupils with special educational needs;
- an evaluation of policies for special educational needs and the effectiveness of the curricular and other provision which stems from them, in terms of assessment of individual needs, differentiated teaching, meeting the requirements of statements for those pupils concerned and effective use of external support services;
- drawing on this evidence, any key points for action in relation to pupils with special educational needs.

CONCLUSIONS ON PERFORMANCE INDICATORS

It is fair to say that organisations such as schools which are essentially about personal relationships cannot be run like machines. Performance measurement is more than an adjunct to the school's values, mission, planning for development and effectiveness, as Tomlinson (1992, p. 55) maintains: 'Performance management is too powerful a tool to be tacked on at the end, its power can be destructive or constructive, dependent on whether it is used at all, and on whether there is consent about values and beliefs in the organisation'. He goes on to say that 'performance management can be a vehicle which carries schools onto greater success in teaching and learning or it can be merely another load to be carried'. The fear is that the way it is being introduced in schools tends to the latter, and extra baggage being carried can only result in less attention being given to teaching and learning. The choice is there to be made and it is a real one.

As a consequence of schools, services or authorities articulating their values and mission, they may work out a development plan and become known for their quality, effectiveness and performance; they will then want to market their product to their consumers. Marketing factors may well influence early developmental planning, as a marketing audit will reveal. Whatever, marketing, in a market economy within the public services, is becoming increasingly necessary.

8

Marketing services for special needs

Virtue does not of necessity bring its own reward.

THE NECESSITY TO PUBLICISE PERFORMANCE

In the light of the above quotation, schools and services, no matter how good they are, need to let their clients and prospective clients know how virtuous they are.

With league tables being circulated by central government on school examination performance, it is imperative that LEAs, schools and services are pro-active in the presentation of their own performance. The range of factors that constitute the effective school are considerable and all schools and services will want to present themselves in the best light. As a consequence, there is a need to be positive in presenting the strengths of schools and services in an ever-competitive environment. As parents are increasingly able to shop around for schools and as schools can shop around for services with delegated budgets, both will need to be active in this market situation in order to market their services.

Marketing theory and practice does not fit easily into the education system. With a long-established 'captive' client group there has been no traditional need to promote a school. Nevertheless, schools and services, and indeed LEAs, have built up a reputation with their clients which has become accepted by communities. Parents evaluate a school on their own criteria and choose one for their children, particularly in the independent sector, on a range of criteria, and this is true for special schools as well as ordinary schools. Dennison (1990, p. 10) listed the following as factors in parents' choice of schools:

- how many of our children attend the school because it is convenient, i.e. no decision has been made?
- how many children attend the school following a positive choice, even though it is convenient, i.e. other schools were considered but rejected?

- how many children attend the school, although other schools are more convenient, which would have represented a more natural choice?
- how many children, where a choice in favour of this school would have been convenient and natural, are being educated elsewhere?
- what are the factors which influence these choices, particularly the positive decisions demonstrated by the answers above?

THE NEED TO BROADEN THE MARKET BASE

With accelerating local management of schools, services will not be able to rely on historic factors for recruitment and employment but will look to extend their markets and services in an increasingly competitive environment.

This raises moral issues, as we have indicated earlier, and challenges the value system of schools and LEAs especially in the special needs sector. Phrases such as the 'competitive edge', 'at the leading edge', are already current in educational circles and a number of LEAs have positively presented their services to their neighbours as examples of good practice and set up management agencies for developing their ideas, as has Cambridge with the SIMS software packages. A number of other authorities in consortium are offering a package of management training in their region, such as Schools Management South, in developing regional programmes. In higher education such as the London Institute, bespoke programmes for staff development have been advertised for schools and services. There have also been developments in this area by the trade unions, as seen in the agency set up by the National Association of Headteachers. The old maxim 'it pays to advertise' has never been more relevant as now in education.

THE NEED TO REFLECT THE MARKET: 'IF YOU CAN'T BEAT THEM JOIN THEM'

Schools are rushing to attract academic and middle-class families, according to researchers at the Open University, even though schools have no evidence of what parents want from them. A three-year research project sponsored by the Economic and Social Research Council under the directorship of Professor Ron Glatter, is looking at 'schools in competition with one another' (Glatter, 1992). Glatter suggests that some schools are attempting to attract parents by changing the way the school operates, altering teaching styles, setting according to ability and building up extracurricular activities. Many schools have no hope of getting a large number of bright children because of their catchment area, but the fight is on to ensure that they attract a significant number in order to make a tolerable showing in the exam league tables.

Certainly the publication of league tables has touched a nerve in education and the country at large, but, as was indicated earlier, these tables are only one indication of a school's performance. As a consequence of this, several LEAs are advertising in newspapers to counter the trend and to overcome bad publicity. Others intend to leaflet parents or release alternative value-added tables to measure how effective schools have been in improving pupils' performance. One example is in Leicester, where secondary schools have adopted newspaper advertising to counter expected bad publicity. Entitled *Celebrating Success*, the advertisement showed the range of work done by schools and deflects attention from raw exam results. Nottingham LEA has also circulated leaflets to parents and advertised in local newspapers, comparing the publication of raw exam tables to 'football results'. So as a consequence of publication of exam results many LEAs are working on the publication of value-added tables of their own.

THE PRINCIPLES OF MARKETING

With management principles and practices being developed throughout the educational system, and with a competitive market descending upon the local management situation, there is clearly a demand for the practical application of marketing principles. As development planning becomes a way of life for schools and services, these plans have to be presented in acceptable form to the various stakeholders in the system. As performance indicators are evaluated, they too need to be reported. All these activities call for a policy on marketing the plans and performance of schools and services. As schools look for potential customers they will need to put their wares 'in the shop-window of Education'.

So what is marketing? It is not necessarily about selling a product; it is about identifying the nature of the product required, ensuring that it is delivered and that every facet of the organisation contributes to the quality of the product.

Marketing at its simplest is the process of matching the abilities of a school or a service to the needs of its stakeholders, so that both get what they want.

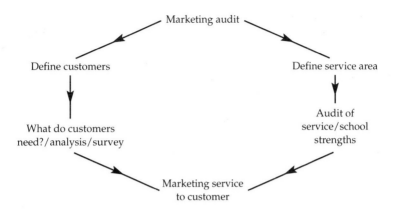

Figure 8.1 *Marketing audit*

THE MARKETING PLAN

As with school and service development, so with marketing there needs to be a marketing plan. Such a plan will also require a marketing audit (see Figure 8.1). Amongst the questions that such an audit will need to address are: what is the marketing environment in which we are operating, who are the clients, and what are we offering?

In developing a marketing audit in Clwyd for the schools psychological service, the central special needs team reviewed the environment in the county for service support and looked at the legislative trends facing the education service. A culture had already developed in delegating and contracting services for school meals and transport, with the careers services also taking an agency role. A consumer evaluation survey was undertaken with a sample of schools, a sample of parents and a cross-section of other agencies through a questionnaire. Questions were asked on the extent of contact and the range and type of contacts made. Some of the points received from the schools sample are shown in Table 8.1. Suggestions for service improvement are given in Table 8.2.

A similar internal audit is of course needed for a school or any other service in defining the capacity of members of the work-force and their strengths and weaknesses in meeting the demands of the customers. An audit of the marking activity and marketing system therefore needs to be undertaken. Most LEAs in redefining and reviewing their policy plans in the light of LMS(S) and the requirements of Circulars 22/89 and 7/91 have undertaken an audit of service and school provision. This has been done so that resources can be provided on an equitable formula basis either for delegated

Table 8.1 *Service audit analysis*

Give more time to schools for:	Primary	Secondary	Total
INSET			
Counselling			
Follow-up	31	13	44
Direct action in classroom			
Parents, etc.			
Reduce delays	14	1	15
Increase staffing	12	1	13
Contract visiting	–	5	5
Increased team working	9	5	14
Increased responsibility for directing resources	8	–	8
More direct advice on programmes	9	–	9

Table 8.2 *Service audit outcomes*

	Primary	Secondary	Total
Work with parents	12	7	19
Speed and efficiency	5	4	9
Multi-disciplinary/team work	10	4	14
Assessment (e.g. for statements)	10	6	16
Advice/guidance re children (programmes, management, etc.)	31	13	44
Counselling	–	3	3
INSET	3	1	4
Professionalism/empathy	–	4	4

services or for special needs staffing allocations to both mainstream and special schools, as noted in an earlier chapter.

Individual members of schools or services can undertake self-analysis in terms of a personal audit in those areas which are needed for successful marketing services. On school or service development training days, staff can be encouraged to analyse their performance in key areas of school or service presentation, such as paying attention to parents' needs and feelings, working steadily with no oversight from managers, and generating enthusiasm for service tasks. Once audits have been undertaken in whatever form, a marketing plan can be drawn up. There are several factors in such a planning process, as outlined in Figure 8.2.

In setting objectives, the 5Ps of marketing need to be clearly addressed. These are: the product or service being offered; the price of the service in terms of time and resources; the place where the service is to be offered, i.e. a unit, an outreach support, a peripatetic provision; the people to whom the service is to be offered, pupils, parents, other agencies, schools, teachers, etc.; and lastly, the promotion of the service through a clear articulation of what is on offer

Figure 8.2 *Marketing plan*

through a mission statement, an attractive package, or advertising through meetings the strengths of a school or service by reference to successful performance indicators.

MARKETING A SUPPORT SERVICE

An example of a marketing audit for a support service is given below:

- *The product*
  A service aimed at mainstream schools where pupils are experiencing any difficulty that restricts their access to their statutory rights in receiving the National Curriculum, combining a working partnership of multi-disciplinary agencies with flexibility and problem-solving strategies.
- *The price*
  Time, resources, expertise – training and qualifications, staffing, budget – LMS formula funding. These issues are all addressed within the credibility of the service in marketing 'the right image.
- *Promotion*
  Clear articulation of what the service has to offer in an attractive package. Broad and clear dissemination through regular meetings to which all involved are invited both in-house and out in the community.
- *The place*
  A resource base (central) from which to provide the support. Catering for small groups with specific learning difficulties within the centre itself. Also a peripatetic facility for supporting staff and pupils within mainstream school.
- *The people (customers)*
  LEAs – key personnel, staff of mainstream schools, parents, pupils, governors, headteachers, other support agencies, such as social services, area health.

PRESENTING THE MARKETING PLAN

In the Clwyd authority, a promotion pack entitled *Into the Future* (Clwyd County Council, 1989) was developed which contained the county value system and mission statement, detailed the service aims and objectives and provided a four-year business plan. This was made available to all schools, governors and parents and was promoted by a series of teacher–parent–governor meetings held across the county. The key objective was not only to promote the vision for the future but to bring together all the stakeholders into the common purpose of the education authority at a time of increasing delegation of responsibility to the local level.

Similarly, as school and services assemble their development plans, they will increasingly provide them in brochure form and will want to disseminate their ideas and plans to as wide a constituency as possible and in a form that is easily understood. A word of caution here before going into print: it could be said that people in education produce far too much printed material. Before the school or service commits itself to a glossy brochure, ask the following questions. Who is your audience, do they need this information, does the information need to be sophisticated or simple? Whatever the amount or format, printed materials need to look professional and to reinforce the service image. This goes for a variety of communication materials including letters to parents and other professionals, brochures, information leaflets and newsletters. The language of written communications needs to be appropriate. Several trials with consumers were undertaken in producing a handbook for parents on special needs in Clwyd before an acceptable format was reached. The language used needs to be clear and jargon-free. There is a need to explain things fully. The readers may not know what an IEP or EP means or does, or even what SEN is supposed to mean. As the Parent's Charter on special needs issued by the Department for Education shows, for many schools a brochure or guide-lines for parents will need several translations into the languages of the parents. Should they not also be available in Braille or on audio-tape? Some schools have developed videos demonstrating their activities and provision. It may be advantageous to create a school or service image and house style in developing promotion materials, so that all communications reinforce the image you are trying to create. The purpose of the document or booklet should be made clear in the introduction and a good layout allows the clients to access the information that they need. Any illustrations or photographs should illustrate the point the booklet is trying to make. For example, children's simple line drawings were used to illustrate the points in the Clwyd practical handbook for special needs.

PROMOTING THE IMAGE IN MARKETING

In promoting a service or school the place element may be vital, especially if you are able from the outset to choose the resource base. Most marketing experts would say that the three most important 'Ps' in marketing a product are 'place', 'place' and 'place'. Schools have usually had the place chosen for them locally, but in the case of special schools there is a need to make it clear to users where it is to be found. Is it clearly signposted, or does a map need to be provided for parents? If it is a service with a base within other provision, does it have a name board, is it welcoming, is it clearly visible from the road, and does the hedge need cutting? Having found the school or service, are the signs clear so that people know where to go to the reception, for example? Is the car-parking facility clearly identified? In a multi-lingual setting is attention paid to the signposting? Are the toilets, fire exits and access for the disabled all clearly marked? Attention to such detail overcomes some of the anxieties that parents often feel when they come into school buildings.

Further aspects of the place image are that there needs to be a co-ordinated approach to the environmental design in terms of paint-work, carpets, use of display boards and artwork, and a comprehensive approach to tidiness, litter and noise. Some parents' performance criteria for school effectiveness are more often found in the cleanliness of the environment, tidiness of rooms and the 'appearance of staff'. An attractive environment need not necessarily be expensive. Having entered the building and hopefully found the reception area, is it a pleasant place where visitors can wait and be met by a friendly co-ordinator-receptionist? Getting past the first post has been so often a major ordeal for many parents in the past. Such people need to be warm, helpful and sympathetic, not only at the reception point but also in using the telephone in dealing with enquiries. Over the years, in dealing with parents and professional colleagues, I have attempted to develop a relaxing reception area where visitors can sit in comfort with provision for tea or coffee. Within this environment the image needs to be 'welcome', where visitors feel at home and at ease. In promoting the service image, existing clients often provide the most effective marketing route. So all staff at every level must ensure that the present job is done properly and that parents or schools appreciate that it was done properly. Another factor in service promotion is the need to keep a high profile to clients and from time to time offer further or new services. It is an axiom of effective marketing that everyone is responsible for selling the service in showing integrity and professionalism, in developing time and energy beyond the minimum requirements, and making effective contacts with new and prospective clients.

A support service in particular needs to have a policy on telephone enquiries, which can be a major source of business. All members of staff need to be aware of the service policy in dealing with enquiries over the telephone. Staff may well need appropriate training in dealing with such enquiries and it may be worth having a prompt sheet next to each telephone with adequate information, so that people can deal effectively with incoming calls. It may be that a standard form can be developed to record all enquiries and messages. Services could consider a time limit for responding to enquiries and installing answerphone facilities when no member of staff is present, or where only a part-time receptionist is available in school or service base.

In preparing a promotional plan for a support service, the needs of the LEA, the service and the schools will vary, as will the direction of the service, depending on the differing constraints.

VARYING FORMS OF PROMOTION

The forms of promotion can be roughly separated into indirect contact via promotional materials and media coverage and direct contact with service users.

Examples in the former area may include brochures and booklets highlighting service strengths and skills, advertisements in newsletters, or leaflets to schools, or even promotional videos outlining a service activity. A three-sided leaflet entitled *Pocket the Facts* produced in Clwyd highlighted a service range of activities, costs and personnel which would fit easily into a top pocket. In the latter area, media coverage in the newspapers and on television or radio is very relevant. A particular example was of an educational psychologist on a local radio phone-in, which brought a very vigorous response of enquiries. The parent's action line (PAL) and its use of British Telecom has certainly been a fruitful media contact for special needs. The use of the media by the independent and voluntary organisations in special needs is another good example. Direct contact with clients via parent evenings, conferences or show-case sessions for special needs co-ordinators or governors are useful, as is the value of networking through existing clients and professional groups and associations. Such ideas need to be targeted, programmed, costed, entered into the developmental plan, and then monitored.

'CORNERING THE MARKET'

With regard to the product, the market survey undertaken by the psychological service in Clwyd highlighted a number of areas where work was only satisfactory or could be developed or improved. Under delegation of services, contracts have already been struck for inservice programmes on school organisation and school development planning. There was a strong indication that staff in schools would welcome more guidance on how to manage disruptive behaviour in the classroom setting.

In marketing their development plans, schools will advertise their quality programmes in terms of performance indicators, in effect their 'product'. So special schools will indicate their emphasis on differentiated, individual, educational programmes for all children. Further, their low staff ratios, advanced educational equipment and specialist provision, such as hydrotherapy or special care facilities, will be highlighted. Others may well advertise their links with mainstream schools and their outreach integration programmes. Still others may emphasise their parental involvement projects at pre-school, or industry and vocational links at post-school. Other schools will advertise their community links and the availability of the school for community projects. The possibility of developing school premises for a range of activities for lettings and events under local management or grant-maintained status is considerable in terms of raising revenue.

In the changing educational environment of the 1990s there are increasing opportunities for schools and services to respond to change in varying ways and to diversify their 'product' base, especially in support services in psychology and special needs. The growth in demand for support for children with behaviour difficulties, with dyslexia problems and for increasing programmes for enrichment for the able within the National Curriculum, presents opportunities for service development. With the increasing competition of league tables many schools will look to the outreach dimensions of special schools to provide expertise in differentiated and individual education programme planning. Finally, advisory and inspection services within authorities will be in direct competition with independent agencies for school inspection contracts. This will require increasing promotion of attractive service contracts at the right price, at the right time, in the right place with the right product.

—9—

Implications for the future

The future is not what it used to be.

(Bernard Levin)

THE MARKET APPROACH

For the immediate future, the market-driven approach to education set out in the White Paper *Choice and Diversity* (DFE, 1992a) has major implications for children with special needs. The market will be clearly selective as competition and contestability sets in and schools become more 'selective' about their intakes. Meanwhile, LEAs are expected to protect the special needs population whilst at the same time delegating responsibility to schools. Left to itself, the education market will work against integration.

Housden's (1992) view of the future for special needs is one of an impending crisis. He sees a future where the local education authority has declined in influence, with a landscape of largely autonomous schools competing for pupils in differing specialist areas. He sees selection becoming rife as schools compete in the market for desirable pupils to improve their ratings, leaving the many to fend for themselves in under-resourced alternatives. In such a climate, he feels that children with special needs are very much at risk with only a weak LEA to assist in charting their course through the market-place of public education.

VALUES IN THE MARKET-PLACE

As we have seen in this book, such a market approach in education presents a major problem for special needs. The problem lies between the tension of market forces versus the need to provide educational access for all. It is clearly seen in the fact that children with special needs have less to invest, yet they require greater investment. Left to market forces, such children will find it more difficult to place their investment. Housden's (1992) view is that with increasing exclusion and segregation, the reality of education as a universal public service is at stake.

The fact that, in the final readings of the Education Bill 1993, much of the attention was focused on those 29 sections concerning special needs, shows concern at the highest levels, particularly about the criteria for statementing. The question of values lies clearly at the heart of this matter. As we have shown, these value questions need to be transferred into mission and policy. This can only be done at the local level, but the climate is becoming increasingly difficult, as LEAs are caught between their statutory responsibilities for special needs and the increasing autonomy of schools.

Values determine educational approaches to quality, accountability and performance. Monitoring these factors has until now been the responsibility of local education authorities, but with their diminishing role there is a danger of a value vacuum being created.

ALTERNATIVE MANAGEMENT STRUCTURES FOR THE FUTURE

In the longer future, the Schools Funding Agency will take over local authority responsibility for many school activities and, as Jones and Stewart (1992) point out, will eventually assume responsibility for ensuring that all children attend school.

In New Zealand, a special education service is being considered as an independent crown agency to employ specialist staff to provide services to schools. A similar service could well cover the role of psychological service in England and Wales, if and when LEAs no longer become responsible for such services, or at least to the increasing number of grant-maintained schools. Such a service would provide for continuity and overcome the criticism of lack of co-ordination and priority of provision.

In the meantime, we could be entering a period of what Mitchell (1992) has called 'contestability in educational services', as seen in New Zealand. This is the development whereby services which hitherto had been controlled by an authority or sponsored monopoly are exposed to competition from a range of providers including those from the private sector. This is mirrored in England and Wales in the development of grant-maintained schools versus independent schools, and the tendering for services by the private sector of previously held local authority and government services. Large sections of the Civil Service have been privatised, with the latest example being the inspection of schools. The growth of private consultancies and agencies bidding for former local authority work in special needs support is evident. Voluntary organisations such as Barnardos and Mencap have for some years entered into joint schemes with local authorities. This could grow, with other organisations such as the Dyslexia Institute, offering assessment and support services to schools.

THE LOCAL AUTHORITIES' RESPONSIBILITY FOR SPECIAL NEEDS

For the immediate future, however, there is still a role for LEAs in the field of special needs, in fulfilling their statutory obligations for identification, statementing and providing education for such children. Indeed, it may be that this is the only role of any significance still left for them for the immediate future. There is however no practical definition, says Vevers (1992), 'of the scope of LEAs' responsibilities in this area'. Even with new guide-lines, LEAs will continue to have an open-ended obligation to an ill-defined group of pupils. Both *Getting in on the Act* (Audit Commission, 1992a) and *Getting the Act Together* (Audit Commission, 1992b) raise key issues on identification, provision and accountability for special needs. Link these to the further issues of access to the curriculum, the amalgamation of special and ordinary schools and increasing technology, and it provides a detailed agenda. Managing these issues and the changing practices of speedier statements and the problems brought about by greater choice for parents, will occupy those in management both at the centre and at the circumference of special needs education for the medium future.

CHANGING EDUCATIONAL VALUES

In the longer term, we are clearly entering into a post-industrial setting with increasing technology taking over many of the roles undertaken by those employed in previous decades.

What kind of educational goals such a post-industrial society will have may well be dependent on the value systems that this society holds dear, and whether such values are quantitative or qualitative. The hyper-expansionist (HE) vision may emphasise masculine priorities, whilst an alternative vision may concentrate on more sane, humane and ecological (SHE) feminine priorities. For education, the HE vision could see education dividing into two main areas. In the first area a person will qualify for a high-status professional élite job. In the second, people will not work but are trained to use their leisure and to accept a lower status. The SHE philosophy could focus on education for capability, helping people to develop life skills. Most people in this vision of the future, as mentioned earlier, might work on a part-time basis but also undertake community voluntary work. Whatever the vision or even a combination of visions, the view that education prepares young people to obtain qualifications for a full-time job in a period of mass employment is over. The effects of these factors upon schooling and the curriculum are clearly apparent in a time of rapid change.

MANAGEMENT OF CHANGE OR CHANGING MANAGEMENT?

All management is about the management of change, and a major change needed for the future is in the area of maximising school effectiveness for special needs.

An integrated model for the management of change has been approached in this book and applied to special needs. The success of such a model for myself in Clwyd, with the pressures brought about by the Education Acts 1981 and 1988, depended greatly on co-operation at all levels, particularly at the local level, in giving a clear vision and lead, with a sense of mission allied to a clear policy. This promoted a partnership between the authority and the schools so that a culture with common aims and objectives in the special needs field became established. This culture of co-operation was found not only in schools and services but also with parents and with the wider community. The transfer of this model of collegiality in the development of effective schools is necessary at the school level. So as we have seen, common aims and objectives need to be articulated through development planning and performance indicators. The issue is not only to manage change but to change management practices. 'Changes require a new culture and philosophy of the organisation of education at the school level. They are more than purely financial, they need a general shift in management' (Coopers & Lybrand, 1989).

MANAGEMENT SKILLS AND STRATEGIES

The management of change includes positive measures such as flexibility, innovation, progression, renewal and the ability to take risks. Change can be planned or unplanned, intentional or unintentional, slow or rapid; whatever, change involves organisations and structures. The key issues underpinning the effective management of change in special needs is not only to respond to what is imposed by legislation but to create opportunities for those involved. All participants in the change process must not only feel involved but feel that

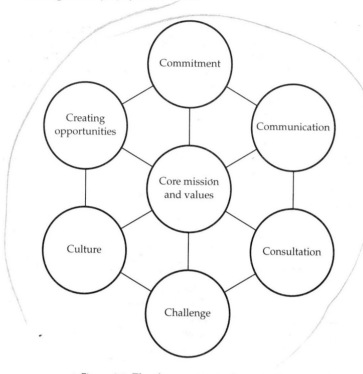

Figure 9.1 *The change process: the seven Cs*

they have influence over the changes which are taking place. This implies collaborative management, joint planning, whole school and service consultation and involvement (see Figure 9.1). In all of this, the concept of the self-managing effective school is firmly on the change agenda.

Nevertheless, change, however initiated or supported, is invariably slow and difficult to measure, causing conflict and tension to those involved. The effect of the change process cannot be accurately predicted because each situation is unique in itself. Despite these complexities Ainscow (1991), Ainscow and Muncey (1989) and Bowers (1985), amongst others, point out that schools must adapt themselves to the demands of the system if they are to remain operationally effective to survive. Strategic special needs issues for the self-managing school are the whole school approach to integration, curriculum differentiation, and effectiveness of support networks, as shown in an earlier chapter. Ainscow and Florek (1989) appropriately defined the term 'whole school approach' as 'an attempt to utilise all resources of a school to foster the development of all its children'. The word 'all' symbolises the principles of sharing, joint exploration, networking, collaboration and continuity, together with progression, all to be reflected in the overall management of the school. This approach seems to be a suitable operational framework for managing change and could be used as the base to develop an effective model for achieving and managing integration.

What has to be acknowledged is that there are many barriers to creating schools which are able to incorporate new demands and resultant changes as part of the normal organisational life. It is therefore crucial to identify and examine these obstacles, so that appropriate strategies can be developed that are not only theoretically sound but practically viable in managing change effectively within schools.

In order to adopt and adapt to new demands and ways of working it is necessary for all those involved, not only within the school but outside – parents, LEA, community, support services – to have a reasonably clear understanding of what, for example, integration is, how it is to work within the whole school approach, the purpose and outcomes and how it will affect those who are participants. It is thus crucial that discussions, plans, ideas and strategies need to be collaboratively developed and communicated, allowing for maximum opportunity for interaction.

Lack of preparation or insight on the part of management regarding staff, community and pupils' needs and attitudes may result in an organisational drift far from effective change. It is important, as I indicated earlier, that the school's vision or mission and central values are accepted by the staff, thereby forming a cohesive school culture. For example, these values could be those of equality, equity and quality education. It is the task of the organisational structure to promote and facilitate participation and a free exchange of ideas and co-ordination between all the members. In this context, the role of special educational needs co-ordinators can be of immense value, as they become the central co-ordinating point for various exchanges and activities and key agents for change.

'KEY PLAYERS' IN SPECIAL NEEDS MANAGEMENT

The possibility of using specialists as 'facilitators' or 'change agents' in overcoming the gap between special and ordinary schools and for 'integration' has been endorsed by a number of researchers (Bowers, 1985; Hanko, 1988; Dean, 1989; Dessent, 1989). Appointing a SEN co-ordinator or special needs team, for consultancy, support, liaison and inservice training, can be an effective tool in instigating and managing change. The duties and responsibilities of the facilitator are very varied, and yet crucial to the success of the model. Figure 9.2 brings out this multi-faceted role clearly.

Such co-ordinators do not work alone, but generally operate with a management committee comprised of governors, middle to senior managers in the school, representatives of heads of departments and sometimes support service personnel who visit the schools. These committees are accountable to the governing body of the school for carrying out special needs policy and their work is monitored over a range of special needs performance indicators (as was indicated in Chapter 7).

THE NEED TO CHANGE ATTITUDES

Existing attitudes are a further barrier to improvement or change. Management must identify the so-called 'negative' attitudes and factors within teachers and try to change them through an interactive open approach. Colleagues resisting integration should be viewed as serving a means to examining and questioning the value of the issue in question, rather than be seen as a problem.

So the teaching staff needs to feel valued and important. Handy (1984) mentions four types of valuing teachers within schools: consideration, feedback, delegation and consultation. All these are important techniques in the creation of desirable attitudes.

People may understand and appreciate the need for a whole school approach to integration but feel incompetent to carry it out due to lack of necessary skills, information or knowledge. Adequate time and resources must be allowed for professional staff training and development, as undertaken in Clwyd, before going headlong into any implementation phase. Adequate skills need to be developed in areas such as curriculum transaction and differentiation, preparation of materials, handling equipment and aids and developing new technology.

Working collaboratively in a team or group through frequent inservice training programmes is highly beneficial (Dean, 1989), and more so when the special needs co-ordinator acts as an agent of change.

MANAGEMENT RESOURCES FOR SPECIAL NEEDS

Poor resource management is another key factor working against change. This has practical implications in that attempts to innovate can easily be frustrated due to unavailability or lack of either human, financial or material resources (West and Ainscow, 1991). The problem is further compounded when there is a lack of clarity in what the

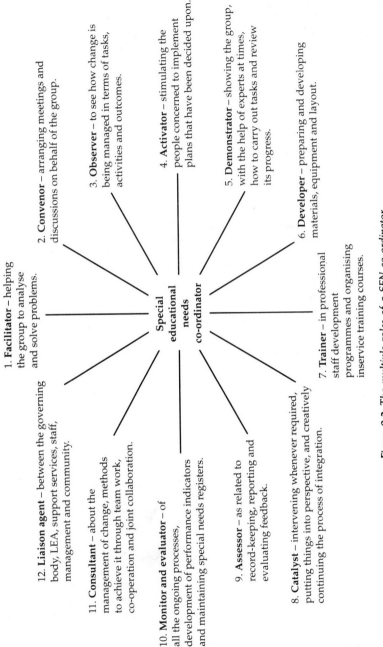

Figure 9.2 *The multiple roles of a SEN co-ordinator*

school desires to do, with inappropriate methods of resource management and a political perspective that dominates resource allocation (West-Burnham, 1990).

There needs to be a balance between control and autonomy, so that the effective school coping with change is enhanced when control is balanced by autonomy (Peters and Waterman, 1982; Handy, 1984). School management needs to be clear in areas such as:

• control of resources;
• centralisation vs. decentralisation;
• financial autonomy of various departments;
• the timetable as related to roles, duties and responsibilities;
• permeation of whole school policies into all areas of operation;
• communication and feedback;
• monitoring and evaluation.

One of the problems with autonomy is that individuals have to take responsibility for their own work. This requires confident, well-trained staff. No organisation can simply move from centralisation to decentralisation without dire consequences, so prior planning and staff preparation is critical.

READINESS FOR CHANGE

A lack of readiness of the school for change is another key area for management attention, as the overall organisational structure may prevent the new way of working from being implemented. It is therefore necessary to check and evaluate the 'readiness' of a school (Huberman and Miles, 1984). As a result of extensive research, Fullan and Park (1981) have drawn attention to teacher input, professional development, principal's actions, board and community support and realisable expectations as major factors in preparing a school for effective change. West and Ainscow (1991) have added the broader ones of clarity of purpose, realistic goals, motivation, support, resources and evaluation, thus emphasising the need for realistic planning.

MANAGEMENT FOR EFFECTIVE SCHOOLING

The question that automatically follows this analysis is, what are the features of the so-called 'effective' school as a result of 'good' change management? To the comments contained in Chapter 7, the following features that characterise exceptional schools could be added. They are:

- the principal's leadership and attention to the quality of instruction;
- heads who devolved power;
- a pervasive and broadly understood instructional focus;
- a sense of mission shared by all, with clearly stated goals and joint planning;
- a positive, safe and orderly climate conducive to teaching and learning;
- teacher behaviour that contains a sense of optimism;
- systematic procedures for monitoring and evaluation.

The above characteristics have been confirmed by Renihan and Renihan (1984); Rutter *et al.* (1979) and Mortimore (1988).

Based on such a detailed identification and analysis of barriers impeding change, strategies can be planned more easily and realistically in order to pave the way for a whole school approach to special needs management.

In order that future developments may be made for effective schools for special needs, there may need to be a change of perspective. Flynn (1990), as mentioned earlier, has advocated the concept of 'inclusion' which looks at the school in overall relation to its community. He sees the school embracing the needs of all the children in its community to a position of complete comprehensivisation. A change of perception is often required so that a problem can be tackled from a different perspective.

Throughout the western world there are change proposals to move from integration to inclusion in the community, to 'society for all'. The All Wales strategy for the mentally handicapped, embracing a 'cradle to the grave' community philosophy, can be seen to be part of this comprehensive community change process.

MANAGING TECHNOLOGY FOR SPECIAL NEEDS

We are now moving into a further round of high technology developments with the advancement of some sophisticated micro-technology. Special needs has already benefited from earlier enhanced technology in computerised devices for differentiation of the curriculum by input and outcomes. The keyboard overlays and sensitive touch-pads are already commonplace, as are increasingly multisensory facilities in special schools. The dyslexic child can have access to a lap-top computer with word-processing and spell-check facilities in most parts of the country.

As the 'chip' technology develops, accessing wider-ranging information is going to be increasingly available. Schools will interact through advanced 'modems' and interactive telecommunications in order to share developments in an increasing sophisticated network of international contacts. There will be a changing role for the teacher from being a communicator to one who starts the communication process, from the one who presents knowledge to the one who learns how knowledge is found. Teachers will no longer impart knowledge, but will allow children to discover knowledge for themselves, a process rather than a product approach. So new technology will open doors to give greater access and opportunity for those with special needs and bring about a 'greater degree of normalisation'.

CONCLUSIONS

Special needs management will inevitably take account of these changes in the future. What is needed is flexibility in the use of the principles and procedures that have been developed in this book, according to the nature of the change that takes place and the changes desired, so that special needs management can be an effective tool in the progress of educational institutions.

On a controversial note, Housden (1992) suggests that the market can be 'bucked' against its pressures on special needs if LEAs combine their moral authority with their remaining statutory functions for education. To this end, they will also need to develop alliances with other service providers, parental groups and voluntary organisations.

On a positive note, it seems more appropriate in looking to the future for special needs to take the optimistic mood captured in the words of Dr Martin Luther King: 'Some look at how it is and ask: why? I look at how it could be and ask: why not?'

Bibliography

Adamson, C. (1992) The windmills of yesteryear. *Guardian Education* (10 November), 7.

Ainscow, M. (1984) 'Curriculum development in special schools: The role of management'. In Bowers, op. cit.

Ainscow, M. (1991) *Effective Schools for All*. London: David Fulton.

Ainscow, M. and Florek, A. (1989) *Special Educational Needs: Towards a Whole School Approach*. London: David Fulton.

Ainscow, M. and Muncey, J. (1989) *Meeting Individual Needs*. London: David Fulton.

Audit Commission (1989) *Losing an Empire, Finding a Role: The LEA of the Future*. Occasional Papers 10. London: HMSO.

Audit Commission (1992a) *Getting in on the Act*. London: HMSO.

Audit Commission (1992b) *Getting the Act Together*. London: HMSO.

Audit Commission (1992c) 'Analysis of special needs provision in Lincolnshire'. In Audit Commission (1992b), p. 46.

Ball, S. (1990) *Markets, Morality and Equality in Education*. London: Tufnell Press.

Bowers, T. (1985) *Management and the Special School*. London: Croom Helm.

Bowers, T. (1989) *Managing Special Needs*. Milton Keynes: Open University Press.

Brent, D. and Burnham, J.W. (1990) *Marketing Schools: Education Management for the 1990s*. Harlow, Essex: Longman.

Caldwell, B. and Spinks, J.M. (1988) *The Self Managing School*. Lewes, Sussex: Falmer Press.

Centre for Studies on Integration (1991) *Fact Sheet: Segregation Statistics English LEAs*. London: Centre for Studies on Integration in Education.

Cheshire County Council (1992) *Learning Support Service: Mission and Policy*. Chester: Cheshire County Council.

Children Act (1989) See Rogers, W.S. and Roche, J.

Clark, A. (1993) *Checklist for Proposals to Extend LMS to Special Schools*. Letter to Chief Education Officers in England. London: Department for Education (18 January).

Clwyd County Council (1986) *Handbook for Parents of Children with Special Needs*. Mold, Clwyd: Clwyd County Council Education Department.

Clwyd County Council (1989) *Into the Future*. Mold, Clwyd: Clwyd County Council Education Department.

Coopers & Lybrand (1989) *Local Management of Schools*: London: DES.

Coopers & Lybrand (1992) *Buying for Quality: School Management Task Force*. London: DFE Publications.

Cumbria County Council (1992) *Policy and Support for Special Needs*. Carlisle: Cumbria County Council.

Danks, C. (1992) 'Outreach programme from Round Oak School'. A consultative paper to the EASE Conference, Davos (October).

Davies, B., Ellison, L., Osborne A. and West-Burnham, J. (1990) *Education Management for the 1990s*. London: Longman.

Dean, J. (1989) *Special Needs in the Secondary School. The Whole School Approach*. London: Routledge.

Dennison, B. (1989) The competitive edge. *School Organisation* 3(2).

Dennison, B. (1990) Performance indicators and consumer choice. *International Journal of Educational Management* 4(1), 8–11.

Department for Education (DFE) (1992a) *Choice and Diversity. White Paper for Education*. London: DFE.

Department for Education (1992b) *Evaluation Criteria for Special Needs*. OFSTED Inspection Manual. London: DFE.

Department for Education (1992c) *Special Educational Needs Access to the System. A Consultation Paper*. London: DFE.

Department for Education (1993a) *Department for Education News* 4/93 (7 January). London: DFE.

Department for Education (1993b) *Department for Education News* 7/93 (11 January). London: DFE.

Department for Education (1993c) *Local Management of Schools and Special Needs*. London: HMSO.

Department of Education and Science (DES) (1978) *Report of the Committee of Enquiry into the Education of Handicapped Children and Young People. The Warnock Report on Special Educational Needs*. London: HMSO.

Department of Education and Science (1986) *Better Schools*. London: HMSO.

Department of Education and Science (1988a) *Secondary Schools: Analysis of the Best Two Hundred Schools*. London: HMSO.

Department of Education and Science (1988b) *Sixty-Six Secondary Schools*. London: HMSO.

Department of Education and Science (1989a) *Planning for School Development*. London: HMSO.

Department of Education and Science (1989b) *The Role of Support Services for Special Needs*. London: HMSO.

Department of Education and Science (1990a) *Developing School Management*. London: HMSO.

Department of Education and Science (1990b) *Staffing for Pupils with Special Educational Needs*. Circular 11/90. London: HMSO.

Department of Education and Science (1991a) *Local Management of Schools*. Circular 7/91. London: HMSO.

Department of Education and Science (1991b) *National Curriculum Development in Special Schools*. London: HMSO.

Department of Education and Science (1991c) *10 Good Schools*. London: HMSO.

Department of Education and Science (1992) *Integration of Special Needs into Secondary and Further Education*. London: HMSO.

Dessent, T. (1989) *Making the Ordinary School Special.* London: Falmer Press.

Doe, J. and Kelly, D. (1992) Performance indicators for governors. *Times Educational Supplement* (16 November).

Dore, D. (1993) Mission statement for schools. *Times Educational Supplement* (6 March).

Eggar, T. (1988) 'Performance indicators: role and value'. Paper to the Industrial Society (September).

Everard, K. B. and Morris, G. (1985) *Effective School Management.* London: Harper & Row.

Fagg, S., Skelton, S., Aherne, P. and Thornber, A. (1990) *A Curriculum for All.* London: David Fulton.

Fish, J. (1985) *Educational Opportunities for All?: The Report of the Committee Reviewing Special Educational Provision.* London: ILEA.

Fish, J. (1989) *What Is Special Education?* Milton Keynes: Open University Press.

Flynn, G. (1990) *A School System in Transition.* Waterloo, Ontario, Canada: Waterloo Region RC School Board.

Fullan, M. (1982) *The Meaning of Educational Change.* New York: Teachers College Press. Rev. edn (1991) *The New Meaning of Educational Change.* New York: Teachers College Press/London: Cassell.

Fullan, M. and Park, P. (1981) *Curriculum Implementation.* Toronto: Ministry of Education.

Glatter, R. (1992) 'Competition between schools'. Unpublished research project. Milton Keynes: Open University.

Gomer, M. and Petrie, I. (1990) *Survey of Support Services.* Stafford: SENNAC, National Association of Remedial Education.

Gordon, V. (1992) *Your Primary School.* Stafford: National Association of Remedial Education.

Guardian (1990) A mission statement by the Church of England. *The Guardian* (27 May).

Halsey, A. H. (1993) Individualism, the root of moral decay. Letter to *The Guardian* (4 March).

Hammond, J. (1988) Education and the consumer. *RSA Journal* (July), 547–56.

Handy, C. B. (1984) *Taken for Granted: Understanding Schools as Organisations.* York: Longman/Schools Council.

Handy, C. B. (1985) *Understanding Organisations.* Harmondsworth, Middlesex: Penguin.

Hanko, G. (1988) *Special Needs in Ordinary Classrooms.* Oxford: Blackwell.

Hargreaves, D. H. (1989) *Planning for School Development.* London: HMSO.

Holly, P. and Southworth, G. (1989) *The Developing School.* Lewes, Sussex: Falmer Press.

Housden, P. (1992) *Bucking the Market: LEAs and Special Needs.* London: Institute of Education, University of London.

Hubermann, A. M. and Miles, M. B. (1984) In West and Ainscow, op. cit.

Jones, J. and Stewart, S. (1992) Choice in education but who benefits?

The role of the school funding agency. *Local Government Chronicle* (September), 17.

Keegan, V. (1991) Pop educational charts are aiming at the wrong target. *The Guardian* (9 September).

Kent County Council (1992) *Guidelines to Primary Schools on Meeting Special Needs*. Kent Education Department.

Labour Party (1991) *Every Child a Special Child*. London: Labour Party.

Lee, T. (1992) 'Local Management of Schools and special educational needs'. Seminar, Institute of Education, London (6 November).

Lincolnshire County Council (1992) *Policy for Special Needs*. Lincoln: Lincolnshire Education Committee.

Lunt, I. and Evans, J. (1991) *Special Educational Needs Under LMS*. London: Institute of Education.

McKinley, G. (1977) 'The 7-S system'. In Peters and Waterman (1982), op. cit.

Maclure, S. (1990) Beyond the Education Reform Act. *Policy Studies* 11(1) (Spring), 6–8.

Manchester City Council (1992) *Draft Policy Statement on Provision for Children with Special Educational Needs*. Manchester: Education Department.

Ministry of Education (1945) *The Nation's Schools*. London: Ministry of Education. Quoted in Young, M. (1961) *The Rise of the Meritocracy*. Harmondsworth: Penguin.

Minnesota Schools District (1989) *Excellence and Equity for Schools*. Minnesota: St Cloud School District 742.

Mitchell, D. (1992) 'Contesting contestability in special education: a critical analysis of special education policies in New Zealand'. Paper to International Conference on Social Justice and Dilemmas of Disability in Education, University of Queensland (11 August).

Mittler, P. (1992) International visions of excellence for children with disabilities. *International Journal of Disability. Development and Education* 35(2), 115–26.

Mortimore, P. (1988) *School Matters – The Junior Years*. Exeter: Open Books.

Mouffe, C. (1988) The civics lesson. *New Statesman and Society* (October), 28–31.

National Curriculum Council (NCC) (1988) *From Policy to Practice*. York: National Curriculum Council.

National Curriculum Council (1989) *'A Curriculum for All'. Curriculum Guidance B*. York: National Curriculum Council.

National Union of Teachers (NUT) (1990) *Local Management of Schools and Special Needs*. London: National Union of Teachers.

Northamptonshire County Council (1992a) *Formula Funding LMSEN*. Northamptonshire County Council Education and Libraries Committee.

Northamptonshire County Council (1992b) *The Northamptonshire Approach: Special Needs Policy Statement. A Consultation Document*. Northamptonshire County Council Education and Libraries Committee.

Nottingham Local Education Authority (1991) *Children First, Policy for Special Needs*. Nottingham: Nottingham LEA.

Office for Standards in Education (OFSTED) (1992) *Framework for the Inspection of Schools*. London: OFSTED.

Parrswood School (1992) *School Development Plan*. Manchester: Parrswood School.

Peters, J.J. and Waterman, R.H. (1982) *In Search of Excellence: Lessons from America's Best Run Companies*. New York: Harper & Row.

Pyke, N. (1990) Stretched out to snapping point. *Times Educational Supplement* (24 April), 22.

Renihan, F.I. and Renihan, P.J. (1984) Effective schools, effective administration and effective leadership. *The Canadian Administrator* 24(3), 1–6.

Reynolds, D. (1992) The effective school. *Managing Schools Today* 15, 16–18.

Rogers, W.S. and Roche, J. (1991) *The Children Act 1989: A Guide for the Education Service*. Milton Keynes: Open University Press.

Rutter, M., Maughan, B., Mortimore, P. and Ouston, J. (1979) *Fifteen Thousand Hours*. London: Open Books.

St Cloud (1989) *St Cloud School District 742 Annual Report* 6 (October). St Cloud, Minnesota.

St George's School, Tunbridge Wells (1992) Integration programme. In *Policy for Special Needs*. Kent County Council.

Saint Paul Education District (1991) *Mission and Policy. St Paul Public Schools*. St Paul, Minnesota: Department of Education.

School Curriculum Development (1987) *Guidelines for Review and Internal Development of Schools*. York: Longman.

Sheppard, D. (1983) *Bias to the Poor*. London: Hodder & Stoughton.

Stewart, J. (1988) 'Is a new management emerging?'. Unpublished paper, Institute of Local Government Studies.

Stewart, J. and Ranson, S. (1988) *Management in the Public Domain*. Local Government Training Board Paper, pp. 1–20.

Stiles, C. (1992) A plan that puts everyone into the action. *Guardian Education* (24 November), 9.

Tomlinson, D.J. (1992) Performance management of schools. *Local Government Policy Making* 19(2) (October).

Touche Ross (1991) *Extending Local Management to Special Schools*. London: HMSO.

United Nations (1975) *Declaration of the Rights of the Disabled*. New York: United Nations.

Vevers, P. (1992) Special needs issues. *Managing Schools Today* 1(6) (May).

Walters, B. (1992) Performance indicators special measures. *Managing Schools Today* 1(6), (May), 21–4.

Walters, B. (1993) Swimming with the tide. *Special Children* (62) (January).

Warnock, M. (1992) Letter to *The Observer* (15 October).

West, M. and Ainscow, M. (1991) *Managing School Development*. London: David Fulton.

West-Burnham, J. (1990) In Davies *et al.*, op. cit.

Wolfsenberger, W. (1972) *Normalization in Human Services*. Toronto: National Institute of Mental Retardation.

Appendix
The Code of Practice on the identification and assessment of special educational needs

INTRODUCTION

Part III of the 1993 Education Act, sections 156–194, specifies the duties of LEAs and school governing bodies in relation to the provision for special needs children and covers matters such as assessments, statements, annual reviews and appeal tribunals.

It will be accompanied, as was the 1981 Act, by regulations and a new element, the Code of Practice, which will develop the responsibility for special needs at the local school level and hopefully provide coherent planning between schools and LEAs in assessment and provision. This is particularly the case for the 18 per cent of special needs children many of whom do not have statements. Because of its statutory nature, schools and LEAs must by law 'have regard' to the requirements of the code and through school policy and annual reports will be subject to OFSTED evaluation as to how the code has been interpreted and developed and if the code has not been followed, what has been applied in its place.

This Code of Practice replaces the guidelines and regulations set up under the 1981 Act and the regulations of Circular 3/83 and the modification to the 1981 Act made by Circular 22/89 arising from the 1988 Education Reform Act.

The emphasis on identification, assessment and recording progress of children with special needs is more detailed than earlier legislation, yet follows the Warnock five-stage model of assessment adopted by a number of LEAs in the intervening years and highlighted in the Audit Commission report *Getting the Act Together* (1992b).

The major difference is in the role of school governing bodies to oversee the task of stages 1–3 identification and provision and in particular the role of the special needs co-ordinator in networking within the school across individual staff and departments and with outside agencies and parents.

The role of the school in this context is to be set out in school policy documents which will highlight its procedures for identification, assessment, provision and the review of children's progress. This will be reported on annually by the governors to meetings of parents.

LEAs enter the process at stage 4 in the assessment proceedings after notification by the headteachers/governing bodies of the nature of the child's needs on a review of stage 3 provision and assessment. The key elements of the Code of Practice are found in six separate parts.

Part I

The principles underlying the code are set out in the form of values and mission. This book has explained the need for values to be articulated at both the LEA and school levels and of the need for mission statements in Chapters 2 and 3.

The fundamental principles of the Code are that

- the needs of all pupils who may have special educational needs whether throughout, or at any time during, their school careers must be addressed; the code recognises that there is a continuum of needs and a continuum of provision, which may be made in a wide variety of different forms;
- children with special educational needs require special educational provision to ensure the greatest possible degree of access to a broad and balanced education, including the maximum possible access to the National Curriculum;
- the needs of most pupils will be met in the mainstream, and without a formal assessment or statement of special educational needs. Children with special educational needs, including children with statements of special educational needs, should, where appropriate and in accordance with the wishes of their parents, be educated alongside their peers in mainstream schools;
- even before he or she reaches compulsory school age a child may have special educational needs requiring the intervention of the education as well as the health authority;
- the knowledge, views, and experience of parents are vital. Effective assessment and provision will be secured where there is the greatest possible degree of partnership between parents and their children and schools, LEAs and other agencies.

Then an overall policy statement gives the practices and procedures arising out of these principles:

- all children with special educational needs should be identified and assessed as early as possible and as quickly as is consistent with thoroughness;
- provision for all children with special educational needs should be made by the most appropriate agency. In most cases this will be the child's mainstream school, working in partnership with the child's parents: no formal assessment will be necessary;
- where needed, LEAs must make assessments and statements in accordance with the prescribed time limits; must write clear, thorough and specific statements, setting out the child's educational and non-educational needs, the objectives to be secured, the provision to be made and the arrangements for monitoring and review; and must ensure the annual review of the special educational provision arranged for the child and the updating and monitoring of educational targets;
- special educational provision will be most effective when those responsible take into account the ascertainable wishes of the child concerned, considered in the light of his or her age and understanding;
- there must be close co-operation between all the agencies concerned and a multi-disciplinary approach to the resolution of issues.

The overriding values, mission and policy are that a partnership is to be struck with parents in providing for their children, to minimise the confrontation of appeals against provision.

It is clear that schools and LEAs will need to provide a policy with appropriate information and guidelines for parents explaining their procedures for assessment and provision. In using such an approach with consultation from the earliest stage with parents, only two unsuccessful appeals were raised in Clwyd in the seven years after the implementation of the 1981 Education Act in 1983. School policies in this area, as mentioned in Chapter 4, will be subject to close scrutiny, not only by parents, but by their LEAs, the Funding Agency and not least OFSTED inspectors.

Part II

The Code of Practice establishes a five-stage range of assessment and provision in which schools and LEAs will operate. This is equivalent to the Audit Commission's 1992 *Getting the Act Together* five-stage approach and echoes the recommendations found in the Warnock Report and used by LEAs such as Northampton and Kent with their closely audited stages of assessment. This provides a clear formula for provision under LMS and LMS (S) and equates closely with the keeping of special needs five-level registers, as seen in Clwyd and Cheshire, where detailed assessment and provision was closely monitored through special needs support teams. The emphasis here places the responsibility upon schools for stages 1-3 in terms of assessment and provision and places the responsibility fairly in the context of a school policy document, annually evaluated by the governing body, which would monitor the policy in respect of the following factors.

The governors' report should demonstrate the effectiveness of the school's systems for

- identification
- assessment
- provision
- record-keeping
- use of outside support services and agencies.

The key person in maintaining and delivering this policy for stages 1-3 is the special needs co-ordinator, who becomes a strategic figure in the school's management system. Amongst the responsibilities undertaken by him or her are liaison with parents, support services, and district health and social services, and involving the child in the decision-making process.

These are seen in the following ways:
For parents

- information giving the school's SEN policy in accessible form;
- showing the support available for children with special educational needs within the school and LEA;
- on parents' rights to be involved in assessment and decision-making, emphasising the importance of their contribution;
- on services such as those provided by the local authority for children in need;
- on any local and national voluntary organisations which might provide information, advice or counselling, and relevant local services.

For the child

- *practical*: children have important and relevant information. Their support is crucial to the effective implementation of any individual education programme.
- *principle*: children have a right to be heard. They should be encouraged to participate in decision-making about their special education.

With the health authority, the SEN co-ordinator will need to ensure the effectiveness of systems operated by the school for:

- keeping medical records of children with SEN;
- drawing together further information that may be available from, for example: a
    child development centre
    general practitioner
    school medical service
    child and adolescent mental health service
    community paediatrician
    health visitor;
- the transfer of relevant medical information between phases, particularly at entry to school at the age of 5;

- ensuring that underlying medical causes are eliminated as a possible explanation for observable learning and behaviour difficulties;
- identifying early signs of abuse, neglect, depression, abnormal eating behaviour, and substance abuse.

With social services

- their mechanisms for liaison with social services;
- how they register a concern about the child's welfare;
- how they collaborate with the area Child Protection Committee with regard to children who are on an At Risk or Child Protection Register;
- how they put into practice any local procedures relating to child protection issues;
- arrangements for liaison with the local authority when a child is 'accommodated' by that authority;
- local arrangements available with regard to the local authority register of children with disabilities;
- information on services provided by the local authority for children in need.

A key factor in deciding what constitute special needs at each stage is the 'trigger', for action, or threshold. So, for example, the trigger for stage 1 is the registration of a concern that a child is showing signs of having special educational needs, together with the evidence for that concern. This would be by any teacher at the school, by a parent, or by another professional, such as a health or social services worker. Such a concern would normally be expressed either to or by the child's class teacher in a primary school, or form or year tutor in a secondary school. The trigger for stage 2 is either a decision following a stage 1 review, or where, following discussions about an initial concern between teachers and parents, the headteacher considers that more intensive intervention under stage 2 rather than stage 1 is necessary. For stage 3 it is either a decision following a stage 2 review, or where, following discussions about an initial concern between the SEN co-ordinator, teachers and parents, the headteacher considers that more intensive intervention under stage 3 is immediately necessary.

At each of these stages the SEN co-ordinator will be responsible for ensuring that a record of action is begun and the appropriate information is collected from whichever of the above sources and includes the school records of attainments and achievements. As a consequence of these procedures an individual education programme or action plan is developed for each child at the appropriate level.

It is stressed that children may not proceed to the next stage, as their needs may well be met and overcome at any of these three stages. As with the keeping of a special needs register, dates for review are sent by the SEN co-ordinator within half a term or at least termly to report on the child's progress.

Finally, at stage 3, the use of specialist intervention from support services is clearly stated. This raises a key issue in the delegation of services to schools under the local management arrangements. Clearly there is seen to be a need for services outside schools to support and advise schools, parents and children, at least at this key stage of need.

It could be added that between-school moderation on 'triggers', or threshold of need is also essential if a quality control moderation is going to be effected.

Overall, there is a need for school development plans to be clear about special needs assessment, recording and provision, as outlined in Chapter 5 of this book, and also for a whole school approach to differentiation of the curriculum (where Parrswood School, Manchester was seen to be a good example).

Part III

Covers the formal assessment procedures for children whose special needs are at stage 4 or 5. This is the area of intervention which is the responsibility of the LEA, and which may lead up to the making of a statement of special needs (sections 165 and 167 of the 1993 Act are the key areas).

- LEAs must identify and make a statutory assessment of those children for whom they are responsible who have special educational needs and who may need a statement.

Such a referral for assessment may come from school, parents or by another agency and shall be undertaken within a prescribed period.

- The period from the start of the assessment (defined by the LEA's serving of a notice under section 167(4)) to the service on a parent of a proposed statement (under Schedule 10, 2) shall be no more than *12 weeks*.
- The period from the start of the assessment to the service of a copy of a statement (under Schedule 10, 6) shall be no more than *20 weeks*.

As a result of the referral information received the LEA will then under section 16, 7(i) of the Act consider whether to make an assessment and write to the parents of their intention.

These procedures follow a similar course of statementing procedures known to readers under section 5 of the 1981 Act, although the time scales are reduced.

- The LEA should *either* serve a notice under section 16, 7(4) informing the parent of its decision under section 16, 7(3) to make an assessment, *or* inform the parent that it has decided not to make such an assessment, within *6 weeks* of serving a notice under section 16, 7(1).

The other parties to assessment are then notified and called to participate in the procedures as they were again under the 1981 Act.

Proformas for assessment clearly need to be drawn up by LEAs and other agencies to reflect their responsibilities in these assessment procedures.

The criteria for undertaking assessment at stage 4 are then set out across a range of special needs, with examples including specific learning difficulties and emotional and behavioural disorders.

Unlike the 1981 Act procedures undertaken in many LEAs, where section 5 requests for assessment for statements were often 'triggered' by only rudimentary information received from schools, the Code of Practice requires the very detailed process of stages 1–3 provision and assessment to be scrutinised. Before making formal assessments, therefore, LEAs will need to examine a wide range of evidence.

There is thus a need for strategic planning across LEAs with individual schools (including grant-maintained schools) and the Funding Agency, for the purpose of moderating agreed criteria for assessment and provision for special needs, with agreed formula funding at each level and appropriate specialist support. Chapter 4 examined many of these issues when considering the impact of LMS upon special needs provision.

Before such special education provision is made, LEAs will require that from the three stages of provision, evidence is provided to show that the appropriate levels of action, monitoring and evaluation are conducted at the school level. This will undoubtedly require a very efficient system of professional monitoring on the part of LEAs and a sufficient range of expertise retained by the LEAs to carry out this work.

What is implied here at each level is that appropriate performance indicators of assessment and provision are undertaken by schools and monitored by both special needs co-ordinators and the local authorities. Chapter 6 of this book has paid specific attention to this area.

The examples given in the Code of Practice of the checks that need to be made across a range of special needs of the quality of provision, not least in curriculum terms, call for a rigour of examination not seen in many local authorities up to the present time and imply the setting of vigorous performance criteria for stages 1–3 provision.

Having considered the evidence, and using the criteria set out in the Code of Practice and stage 4, the LEA will then decide whether formal assessment leading to a statement is required. Again, the views of the parties concerned are critical; some useful proformas for receiving parental views and advice are included in the code.

The coda is added that if parents are advised and supported from the start, there should be few anxieties and disagreements about the draft statement.

Part IV

This considers the drawing up of a formal statement of SEN. The regulations under the 1993 Education Act will more clearly set out the form of assessment. This statement may need additional resources from the LEA to be provided to such children for whom statements are agreed. However, resources will also include the monitoring of children's progress, when statemented, under the annual review procedures.

It is clear that under LMS arrangements as outlined in Chapter 4 of this book, a number of LEAs have already reached agreement with schools as to the level of resources that a school will be expected to provide and will be allocated for special needs provision at the various levels of need.

The Code recommends setting up moderating groups representing headteachers and representatives from health and social services to support the LEA in the consistent administration of decisions and statementing. This is very much like the Kent and Cheshire models of the moderation of special needs audits at levels 1 to 5.

After scrutiny of the procedures and provisions undertaken at stages 1–3, if the LEA decides that a statement is necessary, then the period from the start of the assessment (defined by the LEA's serving of a notice under section 16, 7(4)) of the Act to the service of a prepared statement shall be no more than 12 weeks, as stated earlier. This clearly calls for LEAs to be highly efficient in monitoring the assessment procedures, which in many LEAs have taken considerably longer than this. There may well be a need to increase staffing in terms of psychologists and key personnel available to scrutinise and monitor procedures undertaken at stages 1–3.

The elements of the statement are set out below:

- Placement. The type of school or unit where the special educational provision is to be made, or the arrangements for education to be made otherwise than in school.
- Added to this are the copies of the assessments made by the different agencies which will be included in the appendices A to E.
- Part 3 of the statement will address the curriculum needs of the child under the 1988 Education Reform Act and supplement the provision of Circular 22/89 and that set out in previous regulations.
- With regard to the choice of school the LEAs must explain to the parents how they can express a preference, including the choice of independent schools and non-maintained special schools.
- Parents may express a preference for the school in the maintained sector they wish their child to attend, or make representations for a placement outside the maintained sector. LEAs must comply with a parental preference unless the school is unsuitable to the child's age, ability, aptitude or to his special educational needs, or the placement would be incompatible with the efficient education of the other children with whom he would be educated, or with the efficient use of resources.
- LEAs must consider parental representations and arrange meeting(s) with the parent to discuss them if they wish, before issuing the final statement.
- With regard to a decision not to issue a statement or to amendments or any disagreements with the draft statements, LEAs will inform parents of the rights to appeal to a tribunal.

Where an LEA makes a statement, it shall serve a copy on the child's parent/s and give notice in writing of their right to appeal to the tribunal against the description in the statement of the child's SEN, the special educational provision specified in the statement, and the school named or, if no school is named, that fact. The LEA must also give the parent/s the name of the person to whom they may apply for information and advice about the child's SEN, and where an LEA, having carried out an assessment of a child, decides not to make a statement, it shall write to the child's parent/s with its decision, and give details of their right to appeal to the tribunal against the decision.

Part V

This section addresses the special needs of children under 5 and the provision of assessments and statements for this group.

As with the 1981 Act, assessments of under-5s must be with the consent of the parents. There is a stress here on the need for the LEA to liaise with pre-school support agencies including the health and social services and nursery groups. The value of Portage and pre-school peripatetic services is stressed, particularly for children with sensory impairment. LEA guidance on record keeping for non-educational providers for the under 5s is stressed. There is a key role here for child development centres, LEA nursery and special school under-5 provision. The role of voluntary organisations in supporting parents of under 5s is also clearly stressed. Local authority school services departments must provide written information on the range of services and provision for children with special needs. The value of early intervention and assessment is seen as a key factor. Where children under 5 are receiving LEA provision in a nursery setting, the procedures outlined for schools under stages 1–3 should be paralleled in the nursery provision.

Part VI

This is concerned with the procedures undertaken with the annual review of statements and of the need for more detailed review at 14-plus. This review will be conducted by the LEA and consider closely the provision of a plan for transition from school to continuing education or work. The child and parent/s should be particularly involved at this stage, as should representatives from Careers, the FEFC and social services. Transition should consider proposals from the school, the professionals, the family and the young person.

The review procedures are as follows:

• Where a child has a statement the LEA must ask the headteacher to convene a meeting with the child's parent/s and any other professionals as appropriate and to submit to the LEA a review summary by a specified date before the statutory deadline for the annual review. The LEA will give the headteacher at least two months' notice of the review summary return date. The date of the review meeting should be agreed by the LEA, parents and any other group as appropriate.

In order to effect relevant contributions to the review process, the following procedures are outlined.

• The headteacher, when inviting contributions to a child's Annual Review, must request written reports from the child's teachers, parents and all relevant professionals involved with the child; thereafter, circulate a copy of his or her report, summarising the evidence arising from reports received, to all those invited to attend the review meeting at least two weeks before the date of that meeting.
• The headteacher must at this point invite any additional comments and contributions to the annual review, including comments from those unable to attend the meeting.

The review meeting will address the following questions:

- have there been significant changes in the child's circumstances which affect his or her development and progress?
- what are the educational objectives for the child's educational progress during the coming year? What are the long-term aims?
- is any further action required and if so, by whom?
- are any amendments required to the statement?
- what are the parent's and pupil's views of the past year's progress and their aspirations for the future?

As a consequence of the review procedures, the following outcomes are recommended.

- The headteacher (or LEA if the child is being educated otherwise than at school) must summarise the outcomes of the review meeting, setting out any educational targets for the coming year and circulating this report to all concerned in the review (including the LEA, parents, pupils and any relevant professionals).
- This report must be circulated by the date specified by the LEA in its initial letter to the headteacher.
- The LEA must then review the statement, in the light of the review summary and of any other information it considers relevant, before the statutory deadline for review.

If the review decides that a statement is no longer to be maintained or is to be amended, then the parents will have recourse to appeal under the tribunal system if they do not agree to the changes suggested.

A final word on transition arrangements for students approaching 16 who do not have statements but have special needs at stages 1 to 3. The FEFC will need assessments to be provided so that appropriate provision can be made, and schools will need to liaise with Careers and other relevant services so that appropriate information is passed on to the FEFC, and to local and national voluntary organisations.

This Code of Practice builds on the good practice developed over the ten years since the onset of the 1981 Act in 1983 and heralds a 'new deal' for children with special needs in the schools of England and Wales.

It provides a statutory substance for the framework of management practices and procedures discussed in this book, not least the need for policy and detailed development planning at the local school level.

Name Index

Subject Index